18.7.4

Discovering
Literary
Oxfordshire

Marilyn Yurdan

Also by Marilyn Yurdan
The Sheldonian Theatre, Oxford, Yesterday & Today
A Guide to Family History
Tracing Your Ancestors
Irish Family History
Oxfordshire & Oxford
Oxford Town & Gown
Unexplained Oxford & Oxfordshire

First published August 2003
by
The Book Castle
12 Church Street
Dunstable
Bedfordshire LU5 4RU

ISBN 1 903747 06 6

Designed and typeset by Caroline and Roger Hillier
The Old Chapel Graphic Design

Printed by Print Solutions Partnership, Wallington, Surrey

Front and back cover: High Street, Oxford in the 19th century

Contents

Foreword

I felt it a pleasure and a privilege to be asked to write a brief Foreword for Marilyn Yurdan's new book – and not just because I found myself one of the writers featured in it. No. The far more important reason is that Marilyn was born and bred in Oxford, knows the city and the county intimately, and writes with the same elegance and authority that she exhibited in her splendid earlier work, *Oxford, Town and Gown* (1990).

The present book breaks much new ground in that it covers the whole of Oxfordshire, not just the City and University of Oxford; covers, too, all types of literature from poetry, plays, essays, and novels – to memoirs, crime, journalism, and satire. And, as the clearly and cleverly arranged chapters show, the big boys are not allowed to elbow aside the more obscure and local writers. And it is a huge span that Marilyn covers, from the *Anglo-Saxon Chronicles* to Humphrey Carpenter, from Thomas Bodley to Alan Bennett.

As a Cambridge man, I was interested to note the academic details of those writers who were members of the University, since their specialisms and classes of degrees are given where appropriate. Many did not study English, with their subjects including Classics, Modern Languages, History – even Medicine. More surprising – and sobering – is the discovery that a considerable number of the great (and perhaps not so good) left Oxford without a degree. Amongst such failures we find A.E.Housman, Percy Bysshe Shelley, Walter Savage Landor, Algernon Swinburne, William Morris, and two writers whose work is considered by many to capture the very essence of Oxford, Max Beerbohm and John Betjeman. And that's omitting two of the greatest Englishmen ever born – Samuel Johnson and Edward Gibbon.

For the benefit of literary pilgrims, each entry has a reference to where any surviving connections to that writer may be found within the County – colleges, portraits, homes, burial places, etc. – as well as a series of walks in the centre of the City.

The book is a treasure-chest of information and fascination, and for all of us a passport to the literary delights of Oxford and Oxfordshire.

Colin Dexter, Oxford, April 2003

About the Author

Any writer who works in Oxford, with its history, museums, art galleries and libraries, is fortunate. Marilyn Yurdan is more privileged than most for she has been Assistant Custodian at the University's Sheldonian Theatre since 1984. The Theatre has played host to an astonishing number of literary giants since its opening in 1669, including Lewis Carroll, Matthew Arnold, WH Auden, Grahame Greene, Evelyn Waugh, Iris Murdoch, Martin and Kingsley Amis, Joanna Trollope and Philip Pullman, to name only a few. More personal connections are serving JRR Tolkien when she was working in a bank, having AN Wilson as a colleague in a bookshop, becoming friends with Colin Dexter during the filming of the 'Inspector Morse' series, and meeting Alan Bennett at the Bodleian Library's 400th birthday celebrations.

Marilyn Yurdan was born in Oxford and has spent most of her life in Oxfordshire. She is a graduate of Oriel College where she took a Master of Studies Degree in English Local History. Her previous books include *The Sheldonian Theatre Oxford, Yesterday and Today, A Guide to Family History, Tracing Your Ancestors, Irish Family History, Oxford Town and Gown, Oxfordshire and Oxford,* and *Unexplained Oxford and Oxfordshire.*

The following is a guide as at 2003 to the opening times and entry charges of the principal buildings associated with literary Oxford:

All Souls College, High Street
www.all-souls.ox.ac.uk
Open Monday to Friday 2pm to 4pm (4.30pm April to October)
No admission charge

Balliol College, Broad Street
www.balliol.ox.ac.uk
Open daily 2pm to 5pm
No admission charge

Brasenose College, Radcliffe Square
www.bnc.ox.ac.uk
Open daily 10am to 11.30am (tour parties only)
2pm to 4.30pm (5pm in summer)
Admission charge

Christ Church, St Aldate's
www.chch.ox.ac.uk
Open daily except Christmas Day
Monday to Saturday 9am to 5.30pm
Sunday noon to 5.30pm
Admission charge except for residents of the Oxford Diocese visiting the Cathedral

Corpus Christi College, Merton Street
www.ccc.ox.ac.uk
Open 1.30pm to 4.30pm
No admission charge

Exeter College, Turl Street
www.exeter.ox.ac.uk
Open daily 2pm to 5pm
Admission charge, groups only

Hertford College, Catte Street
www.hertford.ox.ac.uk
Open daily 10 am to noon and 2pm to dusk
No admission charge

Jesus College, Turl Street
www.jesus.ox.ac.uk
Open daily 2pm to 4.30pm
No admission charge

Lincoln College, Turl Street
www.linc.ox.ac.uk
Open weekdays 2pm to 5pm, Sundays 11am to 5pm
No admission charge

Magdalen College, High Street
www.magd.ox.ac.uk
Open 10 October to 20 June 2–6pm
25 June to 30 September noon to
6pm
Admission charge 13 April to 30
September only; free for Oxford
residents

Merton College, Merton Street
www.merton.ox.ac.uk
Open Monday to Friday 2pm to
4pm
Saturday and Sunday 10am to 4pm
No charge for admission to college
grounds; charge for Old Library
tour when available

**New College, entrances in New
College Lane and Holywell Street**
www.new.ox.ac.uk
Open Easter to October 11am to
5pm via New College Lane,
October to Easter 2pm to 4pm via
Holywell Street entrance
Admission charge Easter to October
only; Oxford residents are admitted
free.

Oriel College, Oriel Square
www.oriel.ox.ac.uk
Open daily 2pm to 5pm
No admission charge

**Pembroke College, Pembroke
Square, St Aldates**
www.pmb.ox.ac.uk
Open by prior appointment only
No admission charge

**Somerville College, Woodstock
Road**
www.some.ox.ac.uk
Open 2pm to 5pm
mornings for groups by
appointment only
No admission charge

**St Anne's College, Woodstock
Road**
www.stannes.ox.ac.uk
Open Monday to Saturday 9.30am
to 4pm
Sunday noon to 4 pm
No admission charge

**St Antony's College, Woodstock
Road**
www.sant.ox.ac.uk
Open by arrangement only

St John's College, St Giles
www.sjc.ox.ac.uk
Open 1pm to 5pm or dusk if earlier
No admission charge

Sheldonian Theatre, Broad Street
www.sheldon.ox.ac.uk
Open 10am to 12.30pm and 2pm to
4.30pm (closes an hour earlier in
winter) Opening hours vary due to
the Theatre's being in use for
ceremonies and concerts
Admission charge

Bodleian Library, Broad Street
www.bodley.ox.ac.uk
Divinity School open Monday to
Friday 9am to 5pm,
Saturday 9am to 12.30pm
Charge for one-guided tours which
include Duke Humfrey's Library
and Convocation House

Museum of Oxford, St Aldates
www.oxford.gov.uk,museum
Open Tuesday to Friday 10am to
4pm
Saturday 10am to 5pm
Sunday noon to 4pm
Admission charge

Trinity College, Broad Street
www.trinity.ox.ac.uk
Open 10 am to noon and 2pm to
4pm
Entry charge

University College, High Street
www.univ.ox.ac.uk
Not open to visitors

Wadham College, Parks Road
www.wadham.ox.ac.uk
Open in term time 1pm to 4.15pm,
in vacation 10.30am to 11.45am and
1pm to 4.15pm
No charge

Four
Literary
Walks
around
Oxford

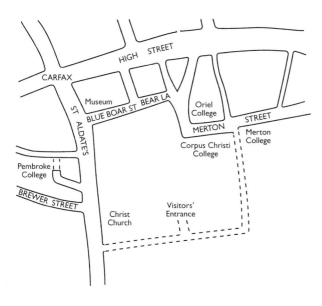

Walk 1:
South from Carfax

Walk down the right-hand side of St Aldate's, noting on the opposite side the former City Library, where *Elizabeth Jennings* used to work; it is now the *Museum of Oxford*.

Continue to *Pembroke College* and its associations with *William Shenstone, JRR Tolkien* and *Dr Johnson*, whose teapot, along with other Johnsoniana, is kept in the Library.

Continue down St Aldate's to *Brewer Street*, where, at Number 1, there is a plaque commemorating the birth of *DL Sayers*. Beyond this in St Aldate's are buildings with Alice in Wonderland connections, principally Alice's Shop.

Cross over St Aldate's to *Christ Church*, with its memories of *WH Auden, Robert Burton, Lewis Carroll, Elizabeth Goudge, John Ruskin, Sir Philip Sidney* and *JIM Stewart*.

Then walk through either Oriel Square or Christ Church Memorial Gardens into Merton Street and *Corpus Christi – Robert Bridges'* college.

Next door is *Merton* and its memories of *Max Beerbohm, Edmund Blunden, Sir Thomas Bodley, TS Eliot, Andrew Lang, Louis MacNeice, JRR Tolkien* and *Anthony Wood*. At one time *Tolkien* lived at 21 Merton Street and *Wood* was born in Postmasters Hall.

Double back to visit *Oriel* with its connections with *Matthew Arnold, Vera Brittain, Thomas Hughes, JHNewman, JIM Stewart* and *Gilbert White*.

On leaving Oriel, go back to Carfax by turning right and walking up Oriel Street, then left into the High Street.

Walk 2: North from Carfax

Walk along Cornmarket, keeping to its right, or east, side and you will reach the church of *St Michael at the North Gate*, where *William Morris* was married and which owns the font from Carfax church where *Shakespeare* stood godfather to William Davenant.

Continue walking northwards, past St Mary Magdalen church and the Martyrs' Memorial and cross over to the pavement to the right. Soon you will come to *St John's College* with its connections with *Kingsley Amis, Edmund Crispin, John Fothergill, Robert Graves, AE Housman, Philip Larkin, John Wain* and *Inspector Morse*.

Cross over St Giles to the *Eagle and Child* where the *Inklings* used to meet.

Continue north on that side of the road, across Little Clarendon Street to *St Aloysius church*, where *GM Hopkins* was curate for a short while.

On leaving the church and turning left, almost immediately you will reach *Somerville* with its connections with *Vera Brittain* and *Winifred Holtby, Dorothy Sayers, Rose Macaulay, Iris Murdoch* and *Nina Bawden*.

The energetic may wish to continue up the Woodstock Road to St Anne's College with further memories of *Iris Murdoch*, and *St Antony's* almost adjoining, which is the college of her husband, *John Bayley*.

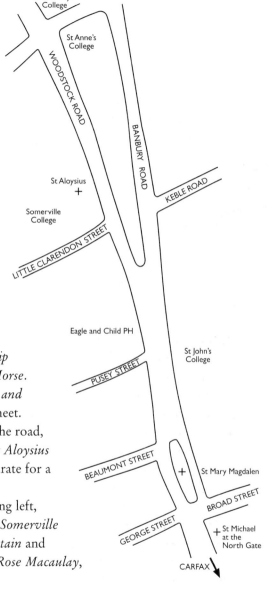

Walk 3: Broad Street

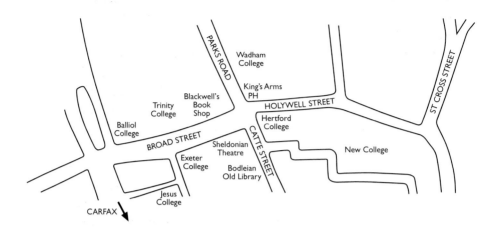

Follow Itinerary 2 as far as the end of Cornmarket then branch right into Broad Street. On the left is *Balliol* with its connections with *Matthew Arnold, Hilaire Belloc, Robert Southey, Algernon Swinburne, Aldous Huxley, Graham Greene, John Evelyn, GM Hopkins* and *Anthony Powell*.

Next door is *Trinity*, briefly the home of *WS Landor* and *Sir Richard Burton*, and more successfully, of *Thomas Wharton, JH Newman, Laurence Binyon* and *Joyce Cary*.

Adjoining Trinity is the main shop belonging to Blackwell's, the world famous Oxford booksellers. Blackwell's offer a Literary Tour of Oxford every Tuesday at 2 pm, Thursday at 11 am, and Saturday at 2 pm. In addition to this general tour, there is one devoted to *JRR Tolkien* which departs at 11.45 am on Saturday and visits locations associated with the writer.

Next door again is the New Bodleian Library and across from it, on the corner of South Parks Road and Holywell, the King's Arms, a home from home for generations of Oxford students. Inside, the walls are covered with photographs of dozens of Oxford worthies, including literary giants. Next door, in South Parks Road, is *Wadham College* of which *John Wilmot, Earl of Rochester*, was a member.

From the 'KA', take a sharp turn to the left into Holywell Street, cross over the road and follow the pavement down on the right side until you reach the main lodge of *New College*. The college has connections with *GV Cox*, *AN Wilson*, and *John Galsworthy* whose commemorative plaque can be seen in the cloisters there.

Retrace your steps back to the south side of Broad Street where you may visit the Divinity School, part of the Old Bodleian Library. Although visitors are admitted to the Library itself only on a guided tour, the Old Schools Quadrangle is worth a visit. In the same complex is the Sheldonian Theatre where degrees have been conferred since 1669 and where the annual Encaenia ceremony takes place.

On the same side of the street is the Old Ashmolean Building, where *JRR Tolkien* worked on the Oxford English Dictionary project, before it became the Museum of the History of Science, and *Exeter College* with its main entrance round the corner in Turl Street. Exeter was home to *Tolkien* as an undergraduate, to *Alan Bennett*, the actor *Richard Burton* on a post-war shortened course, as well as *William Morris* and *Edward Burne-Jones*, whose tapestry *The Adoration of the Magi* hangs in Exeter chapel.

Jesus College, with its connection with *TE Lawrence* and the metaphysical poet *Henry Vaughan*, is further along Turl Street on the opposite side. From there it is a short walk back along Market Street into Cornmarket.

Walk 4: Eastwards from Carfax

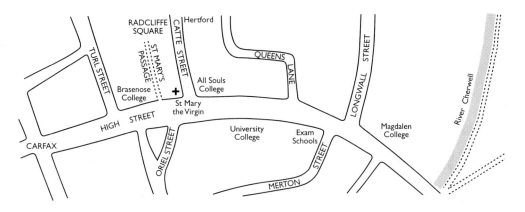

Walk down the left hand side of High Street as far as the *University Church of St Mary the Virgin* where *JH Newman* was curate and thousands of Oxford students have attended services. Follow St Mary's Passage into Radcliffe Square, on the left side of which is *Brasenose College*. BNC has connections with *John Foxe, Walter Pater, William Golding, John Mortimer, John Buchan* and *Jeffrey Archer* and features in *The Adventures of Mr Verdant Green* as Brazenface College.

Cross Radcliffe Square to *Hertford College*; the lodge is in Catte Street which forms the third side of the Square. Members of Hertford and its predecessor Hart Hall include *John Donne, John Meade Falkner* and *Evelyn Waugh*.

Follow Catte Street back to the High Street and turn left to All Souls where *TE Lawrence* (of Arabia) was a Fellow after being an undergraduate at Jesus. Continue on down the High Street and cross over to *University College* where the *Shelley* Memorial can be seen peeping over a crenellated wall. Other 'Univ' connections are with *CS Lewis* and *Sir Roger Newdigate*. Nearly adjacent are the Examination Schools which are not open to the public.

Cross back over the High and continue down over Longwall Street to *Magdalen* with its associations with *Joseph Addison, HJ Pye, CS Lewis, John Betjeman, Oscar Wilde, Compton Mackenzie, Alan Bennett, Jon Stallworthy* and *Seamus Heaney*.

Introduction

This book deals with the present Oxfordshire, taking into account the boundary changes of 1974 by which the county acquired many towns and villages which were formerly in Berkshire. These additions consist of the administrative division of the Vale of White Horse which is centred on Abingdon and Wantage and that part of South Oxfordshire which is centred on Wallingford and Didcot. Along with the places came important literary associations, the principal ones being with King Alfred the Great, Thomas Hardy and John Betjeman.

It is hardly surprising that the county which contains the oldest university in the English-speaking world has connections with a very large proportion of the United Kingdom's leading writers from Saxon times to our own. Some of these Oxfordshire links are tenuous, like Jane Austen's unappreciated stay in Oxford when she was a young girl, Henry James's lodging at 15 Beaumont Street in 1894, Mark Twain's dropping in to be awarded an honorary degree by the University and being uneasy because he was not allowed to smoke, Nathaniel Hawthorne's visit in 1856 when he fell in love with the gardens at New College and DH Lawrence's hobnobbing with the beautiful people of his era at Garsington Manor.

Along with the more classic examples of writers of world renown are included those of more local appeal: Pam Ayres, another import from Berkshire, in the west of the county and Flora Thompson in the north, Anthony Wood and Thomas Hearne writing about the City and University of Oxford as it was in their time. These may not be considered great works of literature (although at one time, Thompson's *Lark Rise to Candleford* was included in the 'O' level English Literature syllabus as an alternative to George Eliot's *Mill on the Floss*) but they are, to varying degrees, records of social and economic history, as well as giving pleasure to thousands of readers over the years.

Another example of local writing, although not strictly speaking literature in the accepted sense, is George Valentine Cox's *Recollections of Oxford* which appeared in 1868 and is a major source of information on Oxford from the late 18th to the mid-19th century. Cox was born in 1786 and went to Magdalen College School. He then went up to New College where he took his BA and MA and stayed on to become Master of New College School, a post which he held for 51 years until his resignation in 1857. Before this, at the age of 20, he had been appointed Esquire Bedel of Law. As an attendant on the Vice-Chancellor at all official functions and on the Chancellor whenever he visited Oxford, Cox was in an ideal position to notice and record everything that went on in both city and University between 1789 and 1860, a period of considerable change. He also held the position of Coroner to the University.

Beyond the scope of this book are the numerous Oxfordshire writers who, although producing writing of a very high calibre in their own subjects, are nevertheless principally historians, classicists, philosophers and theologians rather than poets, novelists or playwrights. Furthermore, it must be stressed that the book is not intended to be a work of literary criticism but rather an account of writers who have been in some way or other connected with Oxfordshire, together with an indication of places or items associated with them.

No account of literary Oxfordshire would be complete without mention of the University and the writers whom it has both produced and attracted. For this reason, a section about the University's English Language and Literature teaching over the years has been included.

For the same reason an outline history of the OUP, the world famous Oxford University Press, is given.

Certain Oxford colleges have produced clusters of poets and novelists at various periods, for instance Balliol, with Algernon Swinburne, Hilaire Belloc and GM Hopkins in the 19th century and Aldous Huxley, Graham Greene and Anthony Powell in the 20th, Somerville, with Vera Brittain, Winifred Holtby, DL Sayers, Rose Macaulay, Iris Murdoch and Nina Bawden in the 20th century and St John's, with Robert Graves, Philip Larkin, Kingsley Amis, John Wain and Inspector Morse also in the last century.

Literature and Oxford University

Until 1893, when English Language and Literature were introduced into the curriculum, the word 'literature' at Oxford referred to the writings of Greek and Roman authors. English was a latecomer to the list of subjects in which students could specialise, the first year in which single-subject examinations could be taken being 1864. The *Oxford University Handbook* for 1962 comments, 'English language and literature was slow in establishing its claims to professional scholarly study because of the dominance of classical studies and the theory, of very doubtful validity, that a good education in the classics sufficed to equip a man for the study of his own language and literature.' For a considerable period after its inception, the English course also included Classical 'Mods' or Moderations. Mods, introduced in 1850, are best described as an intermediate stage towards the Bachelor's degree and are usually taken at the end of the second year of study. The first University (as opposed to college) examinations, now officially called the First Public Examination, are still called Mods in some subjects while others have 'Prelims' instead. This reluctance to abandon the past explains why many Oxford graduates who became writers, wrote on classical or sacred themes.

Today the situation as regards the study of English literature is altogether different. The Oxford English Faculty is the largest in the country and includes a selection of authors from Old English times to the 21st century, or, as the Undergraduate Prospectus puts it, 'from the Beowulf-poet to Salman Rushdie.'

Since the majority of the writers featured in this book were students, a whole range of other literatures have been added to the Oxford syllabus. Greek, Latin and Hebrew are of course still prominent, as are the literatures of the major world languages which are also taught in most other universities. More unusual are those in Czech, Slovak, Catalan, Celtic, Galician, Polish, Provençal, Yiddish, Turkish, Korean, Sanskrit, Tibetan and ancient Egyptian. For the purposes of this book, however, 'literature' will be taken to be 'Eng.Lit.'

The classical influence is particularly evident in the subjects of prize-winning essays. Many of the prizes offered at Oxford are long established, indeed some date back centuries.

The Chancellor's Prizes

The Earl of Litchfield, who was Chancellor of the University from 1762 to 1772, donated prizes of £20 each for compositions in Latin verse and English prose and this practice has been continued by each of his successors. On his election in 1809, Lord Grenville added a third prize, for Latin prose. In 1842, remarks Cox, 'the Prize for Latin Verse was not awarded! that is, not one of the few copies sent in was presentable in the Theatre.' This refers to the fact that, until the 1990s, extracts from prize-winning essays were recited as part of the Encaenia, or honorary degree ceremony, in the Sheldonian Theatre. Cox continues, 'Tell it not at Eton, publish it not in the senior classes at Winchester! On second thoughts, if the talent of Latin versification is to be kept up, tell it and publish it there and everywhere.' The set subject in that year was *Noachi Diluvium* (or Noah's Flood); the same thing happened in 1896 when the subject was *Atlantae Insula*.

English Essay winners include James Anthony Froude of Oriel in 1842, with *The Influence of the Science of Political Economy upon the Moral and Social Welfare of a Nation*. In 1871, the Prize was not awarded for the subject *The Universities of the Middle Ages*. The topic was set for a second time in 1883 when the winner was Hastings Rashdall, who was later to write the definitive work on the subject of medieval universities. In 1880, the English Essay prize went to Walter Scott, Fellow of Merton and relation of Sir Walter. Over the decades, there were several occasions when the Prizes have not been awarded.

The Newdigate Prize

Sir Roger Newdigate's Prize for English Verse was the first permanent benefaction, although before that numerous prizes had been awarded by benefactors whose names are now unknown.

In 1806, Sir Roger Newdigate, a baronet from Arbury in Warwickshire, member of University College, Burgess for the University and Doctor of Civil Law, instigated this prize. It was then offered for 'a copy of English Verse of fifty lines and no more in recommendation of the study of the ancient Greek and Roman remains of Architecture, Sculpture and Painting.' The following year Sir Roger died at a very great age and in his will left £1000 with instructions that £21 from its income should be given annually as prize money. The remainder was to go into a fund for the improvements of the Master's Lodgings at University College. The very inconvenient restrictions originally imposed by Sir Roger were removed in 1827 with the approval of his heir, and since then there has been no precise limitation on either the length of poems submitted or their subject matter.

Although it has been said that winning the Newdigate means the kiss of death for aspiring writers, prize-men include such giants as Matthew Arnold of Balliol, Fellow of Oriel, and future Professor of Poetry, with his poem *Cromwell* in 1843, Oscar O'Flahertie Wilde of Magdalen with *Ravenna* in 1878 and Robert Laurence Binyon of Trinity with *Persephone* in 1890. In 1849, at the Commemoration on 21st June, the Newdigate Prize was not awarded, 'though a great many copies of verses were said to have been sent in.'

Nowadays, as with all the University prizes, provided that entries of sufficient merit are received, the Newdigate Prize is still awarded.

The Professor of Poetry

Henry Birkhead, a member of Trinity College and Fellow of All Souls, who was also a Barrister of the Inner Temple and a Doctor of Civil Law, founded the Professorship. He bequeathed an estate in County Durham to finance his bequest, which came into effect in 1708. Added to the monies from the estate was a payment from Lord Crewe's Benefaction, left by Nathaniel Crewe, Bishop of Durham.

The Professor of Poetry is elected by Convocation for a period of five years, on the expiry of which he seems formerly to have been elected for a further five years; now the time span is for five years only. According to Birkhead's stipulations the incumbent must be at least a Master of Arts or Civil Law, although today, in theory at least, it is not necessary for the post-holder to be a member of the University or indeed even a poet. Besides giving three public lectures annually, the Professor takes turns with the Public Orator to deliver the Creweian Oration, a sort of end-of-year speech delivered at the annual Encaenia in June. It was obligatory for the Professors to speak in Latin until Roy Fuller managed to get the necessary legislation passed for the use of

English instead. Nowadays, the Professor's speech is decorated with puns, gentle satire and other witticisms. Another of the Professor's duties is to choose the subject for the Newdigate Prize and judge the poems submitted.

Earlier Professors, who seem to have automatically held office for 10 years, include: Thomas Warton, friend of Samuel Johnson (1756 to 1766); John Keble (1831 to 1841); Matthew Arnold (1857 to 1867) and Francis Turner Palgrave of *Golden Treasury* fame from 1885 to 1895. They seem to have been elected as much for their oratory and quickness of thought as for actually having composed fine poetry. Nineteenth-century holders included many churchmen and it was not until the election of Matthew Arnold who was the first Professor of Poetry to lecture in English in public, that the position gained its present high profile.

Twentieth-century Professors include Sir Maurice Bowra (1946 to 1951), Cecil Day Lewis (1951 to 1956), WH Auden (1956 to 1961), Robert Graves (1961 to 1966), Edmund Blunden (1966 to 1968), Roy Fuller (1968 to 1973), John Wain (1973 to 1978), Seamus Heaney (1989 to 1994), James Fenton (1994 to 1999) and the present holder, Paul Muldoon who was elected in 1999.

Those eligible to vote for the Professor of Poetry are members of the University's Convocation, which is anyone who has taken an Oxford degree. This brings the potential number of voters to several hundred thousand, but because the votes have to be cast in person and are subject to strict scrutiny, less than a thousand people vote. A low turn out is particularly likely when there is only one candidate as at the last election when Professor Muldoon stood unopposed, but past unsuccessful candidates have included writers of the calibre of CS Lewis and Enid Starkie.

As is the case with other universities, honorary doctorates are frequently conferred on writers who have little or no connection with Oxford, and many of whom come from other countries. Although the usual doctorate conferred on writers is a Doctor of Literature, in the past some recipients were made Doctors of Civil Law. An example of this was Oliver Wendell Holmes in 1909; several other writers over the years received this degree but most of these were members of the University.

At Lord Curzon's installation in 1907, both Samuel L Clemens and Rudyard Kipling received the usual degree of D Litt, as did André Maurois at Lord Halifax's installation in 1934. Clemens' honorary degree ceremony on 26th June 1907 received considerable attention both at home in the United States and in Britain. His tour, including the visit to Oxford, was covered by the London correspondent for *Harper's Weekly.* Clemens had already been lionised at a garden party given by Edward VII and was to be guest of honour at a dinner given by the magazine *Punch,* but it was the Encaenia ceremony which captured the public's imagination. The occasion was much more impressive than usual for this Encaenia was the one following the Installation of Lord Curzon as Chancellor. There were 34 honorands – as opposed to the normal 6 or 8 at today's Encaenia – and other recipients included Prime Minister Campbell-Bannerman, the American Ambassador, General Booth, the sculptor Rodin, the composer Saint-Saens and of course Rudyard Kipling.

The American journalist, who might have been a tad biased, wrote, 'But unquestionably it was Mark Twain who of all the recipients roused the greatest enthusiasm. The whole building broke into a roar of applause when he stood up to be presented to the Chancellor.' The assembly was treated to the once-traditional witticisms which on that occasion at least showed that their perpetrators were familiar with Clemens' work.

'Have you got that jumping frog with you, Mark?' one asked. It must have been a sore trial for the writer to have remained silent while all these comments were fired from the galleries and the Orator spoke about him in Latin. However, he was very conscious of the honour which the University was extending to him and remembered it all his life. His trip was mentioned in many later speeches and, at the wedding of his daughter in 1909, he wore his DLitt gown.

After the ceremony, Clemens was escorted to lunch at All Souls by the citizenry of Oxford who were lining Catte Street and Radcliffe Square.

Kipling's involvement with the University took a typically English and understated form when he went off to Henley-on-Thames where he offered the Oxford Eight support and encouragement which was much appreciated during its training sessions.

Other honorary D Litts are PG Wodehouse (1939), Rabindraneth Tagore (1940), André Gide and François Mauriac (1947), Thomas Mann (1949), Edith Sitwell and Walter de la Mare who was an Honorary Fellow of Keble, (both in 1951), WS Maugham (1952), Elizabeth Bowen (1956), Robert Frost (1957), Pablo Neruda and Siegfried Sassoon (1965), Nadine Gordimer (1994), Margaret Attwood (1998), Muriel Spark in 1999 and John Coetzee in 2002.

The Oxford University Press

Exposicio Sancti Ieronimi in Simbolum Apostolorum, the first book printed in Oxford, bears the date *Anno domini M.cccc.lxviij.xvij die decembris*, that is 17th December 1468. However, this is generally agreed to be one of the earliest typos ever recorded, as it should in fact have read 1478. Between the appearance of this first book and 1486, when printing stopped, fifteen books are known to have been printed in Oxford.

In 1517, printing started again at a press in St John Street (the present Merton Street), near Merton College. This press was in operation for two years, then stopped once more until 1585 when Joseph Barnes started up another press with £100 which he had borrowed from the University. Barnes was given a monopoly in Oxford by an Ordinance of Star Chamber in 1586.

The first charter to permit printing in Oxford was dated 1632 and mentions three printers; an amendment of 1632 allows two presses, together with two apprentices, to each of these three printers. Three years later came a royal charter confirming all the University's printing privileges, including that of printing Bibles.

Soon after the Restoration of 1660 began a long wrangle between the University and the London Stationers and King's Printers concerning privileges, in particular that of producing Bibles. In 1665, when the Court was at Oxford during the Great Plague of London, the oldest existing English newspaper began life under the title of *The Oxford Gazette*.

When Wren's Sheldonian Theatre was opened in Broad Street in 1669, it became the first permanent home of the University Press. The founder of the Theatre, Archbishop Gilbert Sheldon, stipulated that any monies surplus to his endowment should be used for the Press. The type foundry was set up in the basement of the building while the printing was carried out on the floor area. Completed books and paper were stored above this on what is now known as the Attic Floor. Previous to the construction of the Theatre, printers were obliged to hire out premises in which to work.

In September 1669, local historian Anthony Wood of Merton writes, 'Our press being up at the Theater and Dr Fell supervisor and corrector of all books, he made it his designe to correct the English and Latin tongue – as in English 'sic' for 'sick,' 'site' for 'scite,' 'contemt' for 'contempt'. . . 'through' for 'thorough.' He mentions a set of instructions then in circulation entitled 'Friendly advice to the correcter of the English press at Oxford,' dated 1681. However, Wood adds darkly, 'But printing many books without frugality and overseeing and examining accompts, run themselves in debt and were forced to let the Theater to London booksellers, 1678.' Several examples of this practice are recorded in the University Archives.

The inconvenience of using the Theatre for two such dissimilar activities as printing house and ceremonial hall is illustrated by an

Oxford University Press buildings in Walton Street, Oxford

entry for March 1681. The King being in Oxford, the Commons met at the Sheldonian. As a consequence 'All the next morning the printers were removing their cases under the Theater to the Morall Philosophy Schoole,' in Old Schools Quadrangle nearby.

In 1688, the printing presses were taken out of the Theatre for fear that they were damaging the building. The Learned Press went across to Catte Street and the Bible Press to St Aldate's, although the Sheldonian imprint continued to be used. The two Presses were not amalgamated until 1862. The first Specimens of Type published in England were issued from the Sheldonian Press in 1693.

Across the quadrangle from the Sheldonian, Hawksmoor's Clarendon Printing House, now called the Clarendon Building, was opened for use in 1713 and housed both Presses. In 1830, the present building in Walton Street was opened.

Cox, under December 1836, writes 'It was agreed in Convocation to accept the offer of an *annual sum* from the University Press, 'being a surplus over the expenses,' to be applied to the *general fund of the University.* 'What a famous milch-cow, that Press!' he comments. A succession of well known publications followed: the Revised New Testament in 1881, the *New English Dictionary on historical principles* in 1882, the Revised Version of the Old Testament in 1885, the Oxford Classical Texts series from 1900, the *Dictionary of National Biography* bequeathed to the University by Mr George Smith in 1917 and the New English Bible in 1960.

In 1989, the Printing House produced its last book, and closed for business in May that year. Printing continues, however, as Oxuniprint, under a Director of Printing Services.

Chapter One

The Anglo-Saxon Chronicle ✍ *Alfred the Great*

William Langland ✍ *Geoffrey Chaucer*

The Anglo-Saxon Chronicle

Oxfordshire is mentioned in one of the earliest surviving examples of English literature which also contains the first written reference to Oxford itself. This is the *Anglo-Saxon Chronicle* which was started by order of King Alfred the Great, himself a native of Oxfordshire for he was born at Wantage, then in Berkshire. Although writing started about AD 890, it covers events from the coming of the Romans to Britain and compilation continued until the middle of the 12th century. One of the last entries is an account of the meeting at Wallingford between Stephen and the future King Henry I, son of his rival for the throne, the Empress Maud.

It is not strictly accurate to speak of *the* Anglo-Saxon Chronicle as if it were a single work, for it survives in several different editions. These are known as manuscripts A (written at Winchester), B and C (Abingdon), D (Worcester), E (Peterborough) and F (Canterbury), together with a fragment H which was also written in Winchester.

The Abingdon B text was written at the abbey there by a single scribe in the second half of the 10th century and its records run from 60 BC until AD 977. In the second half of the 11th century, it went from Abingdon to Christ Church, Canterbury, where it was extended and amended. Abingdon C text was written in the mid-11th century and the fact that it includes local annals indicates that it was produced there.

Like Oxford, Abingdon was on the border between the Saxon kingdoms of Wessex and Mercia. Its Benedictine Abbey was founded in 690, twice sacked by marauding Danes and eventually completed in about 1170. Its royal apartments were used by numerous monarchs and by the 15th century, Abingdon was second in importance only to Glastonbury among English abbeys.

It was suppressed in 1538 and demolished, much of its stone being sold off until only a few buildings remained. In 1945, however, the remnants were bought and restored by the Friends of Abingdon and are now open to the public from April to September.

Most of the manuscripts which make up the Anglo-Saxon Chronicle are in the British Library, the exceptions being A which is at Corpus Christi College, Cambridge and E which is in the Bodleian Library in Oxford.

For the main part, the entries are in Old English, but later ones are in an early version of Middle English. The names are not known of the scribes who were responsible for actually writing any of the versions of the text, which runs to almost 100,000 words. As a historical source, the Chronicle is less than reliable because one of the reasons it was compiled is the glorification of the Royal House of Wessex and tracing its genealogical descent from ancient heroes. It is, however, invaluable as an example of the Old English language and its development over the years into what was to become Middle English. Documents written in Old English are not common as many were destroyed after the Norman invasion and in any case, official documents were usually written in Latin. Old English was not used for official records after the 1070s.

In addition to its linguistic and literary value, the Chronicle is useful for finding out what towns existed at a given date within the years

Right: Abingdon Abbey Buildings (*Anglo-Saxon Chronicle*)

which it covers and in which kingdom these places were situated. Oxford, for example, was once in Mercia but later became part of Wessex.

In addition to the fact that two of the manuscripts of the Chronicle were written in Oxfordshire and another is housed here, there are numerous references to the county within its pages. Besides the historic first mention of Oxford under the year 912, there are frequent subsequent references, all of which suggest that it was a border town of some importance. The 912 entry refers to the death of Ethelred I and the fact that Edward, son of Alfred, took over 'Londonbyrig and Oxnaforda and all the lands which owed obedience thereto,' in other words the Lower Thames Valley.

In 924, when Edward died, he was followed very quickly to the grave by his son, another Edward, who died in Oxford. Another of Alfred's grandsons, Athelstan, became king and spent Easter at Abingdon Abbey surrounded by his court. This practice of spending major church festivals at Abingdon was continued by many of his successors until the Reformation.

Other Oxfordshire places mentioned in the Chronicle include Kirtlington where there was a great council, 'and there died Bishop Sideman by a sudden death. Then commanded King Edward and Archbishop Dunstan that he should be borne to St Mary's Minster which is at Abingdon; and so too was it done,' writes the chronicler. Thame appears as the place where Archbishop Oskytel, who was first consecrated diocesan bishop at Dorchester, died in 970.

In 1006 the Danish army sacked Wallingford, destroying it entirely. They then spent the night at nearby Cholsey. Three years later, we are told that the Danes took an 'excursion through the Chilterns and so on to Oxford which city they burned and plundered on both sides of the Thames to their ships.' Despite the fact that in 1009 the king, Ethelred, had decreed that the whole nation should be called out so that the Danes 'should be opposed on every side, lo! nevertheless, they marched as they pleased. . . And then, after mid-winter they took their way upwards through the Chilterns, and so to Oxford, and burned the city.'

The queen had fled from the royal palace at Headington, taking with her the young Prince Edward, the Confessor-to-be, and gone to her brother's court in Normandy. In 1011 Ethelred promised the Danes tribute and provisions if they stopped their plundering. By this time, however, they had overrun Oxfordshire along with most of the south east of England. In this instance Ethelred certainly warranted his nickname of the Unready or Ill-advised, as his contemporaries were very quick to point out.

In 1013, the Danish king Sweyne, together with his son Knut, reached Oxford, wreaking havoc as they made their way southwards. The citizenry knew only too well what they were in for and decided that discretion was the better part of valour for, when Sweyne and company arrived in Oxford, the townspeople submitted straight away and handed over hostages, after which the Danes set off for Winchester where the citizens acted in exactly the same way as their Oxford counterparts.

Two years later the Great Council met at Oxford where a number of leading thegns, including Sigeferth and Morcar, were betrayed and murdered by the treacherous Alderman Edric. Ethelred died in 1016 and a few months later his successor Edmund Ironside was murdered at Oxford, so leaving Knut unimpeded access both to the throne and to Ethelred's widow whom he subsequently married.

The year 1018 saw tribute paid to the Danes all over England. In Oxford however, Danes and Saxons agreed to live together under King Edgar's law. Knut came to Abingdon in 1034, the Chronicle informs us, when he gave St Martin's church at Carfax, Oxford, to the Abbey there.

In 1035 when Knut died, the Witan, or Council, was convened at Oxford where all the nobles gathered to decide on his successor. The influential Earl Leofric and almost all the thegns north of the Thames, and the leading men of London, chose Harold Harefoot. His reign was destined to be a short one for, in 1039, Harold too died at Oxford. There is little wonder that a rumour started that Oxford was an unlucky place to be for royalty.

Apart from another meeting of the Great Council in 1065 in order to elect a successor for Edward the Confessor, when Harold Godwinson was elected, there is little mention of Oxfordshire in the Chronicle's later coverage of the activities of the Saxons.

Oxfordshire-related entries continue after the Norman Invasion, however. King Stephen returned from Normandy and held a council at Oxford in 1137. He promptly seized the Bishop of Salisbury and his 'nephews' (in reality his sons), the Bishop of Lincoln and the Chancellor and threw them into prison until they agreed to give up their castles. In 1142, after a period of imprisonment, Stephen was back again, besieging his cousin and rival for the throne, the Empress Matilda, in Oxford Castle from September until December. One historical event which virtually all Oxford citizens know about is how Matilda was lowered down by rope under cover of darkness and made her way on foot some 12 or so miles along the Thames to the safety of Wallingford Castle.

Alfred the Great

Alfred the Great (849 to 899) was Oxfordshire's first accredited major writer, although Wantage, his birthplace, was then in Berkshire.

Alfred was as fine a scholar as he was soldier. His biographer, Bishop Asser, relates how he was taught to read when he was 12 by his stepmother, Judith a Western Frankish princess, who instilled in him a love of learning. Although he was the youngest of his father's sons, he was the ablest.

During his reign Alfred made Winchester, his capital, into a centre for study and learning and attracted scholars to the city to share his love of books. Asser says, 'day and night, whenever he had any leisure, he ordered men to read books to him and he would never let himself be without one of them.'

When he was 39 Alfred learnt Latin in order to translate some of the great works of the day into Old English and make them widely available to his subjects. Among these authors were Bede, Boethius and Gregory the Great.

The importance of Alfred's contribution to the literacy of this country was recognised in 2002 when a grant of £334,698 from the Arts and Humanities Research Board was awarded to leading members of the University's Faculty of English and University College London. They are to focus on the Old English adaptation of *De Consolatione Philisophia* by Boethius. *Blueprint,* the newsletter of Oxford University, states that, 'the English translation of the Boethian text is generally recognised as the most ambitious and significant of the writings associated with King Alfred and his learned circle.'

Alfred also wrote about his position as king, compiled a written account of the laws of the kingdom of Wessex, and lastly, ordered his judges the choice between learning to read and being deprived of their posts. A letter written by Alfred is one of the most important items in the history of English literature for it describes the king's plans for the education of his subjects and for the translation of major works into English. A copy of it which Alfred sent to Worcester survives in the Bodleian Library as MS Hatton 20 and, apart from its insight into Alfred's practices and the state of learning in 9th century Wessex, is an outstanding example of written Old English.

The statue of Alfred which stands in the market place at Wantage is a smaller edition of the one in Winchester where he died. It was commissioned by Lord Wantage and designed and carved in 1877 by Count Gleichen, a cousin of Queen Victoria. On the base of the statue is carved·

Alfred found learning dead and he restored it
Education neglected and he revived it
The laws powerless and he gave them force
The church debased and he raised it
The land ravaged by a fearful enemy from which he
    delivered it
Alfred's name will live as long as mankind shall respect
    the past.

William Langland

It is believed that William Langland (c1332 to c1400), one of the leading writers in Middle English, spent some time in the county at Shipton-under-Wychwood, before he entered the Benedictine monastery at Malvern where he was educated. Langland took minor orders and left Malvern for London where he lived with his wife and daughter in Cornhill, earning his living as a scrivener by writing letters, singing requiems and, on occasions, being reduced to begging.

His alliterative *The Vision of William Concerning Piers the Plowman* was written in three (possibly four) versions between about 1367 and 1386. The poem is made up of a series of allegorical visions, in which Piers develops from a poor peasant into a symbol of Jesus and condemns the social and moral shortcomings of 14th-century England. Langland was able to draw upon his own experience of deprivation to give a ring of truth to his descriptions of medieval poverty.

It is known that the poet's father lived in Shipton-under-Wychwood and it is unlikely that William would never have visited him there.

Geoffrey Chaucer

Similarly, the greatest writer in Middle English, Geoffrey Chaucer (c1340 to 1400) must have paid visits to Oxfordshire. A building known as Chaucer's House can still be seen at Woodstock, but there is no evidence for its having any direct connection with the poet, the Chaucer in the title being his son, Thomas. It is certain though, that Geoffrey would have known the town well from his visits there with the royal household and would stay at the royal manor there. Apart from any trips to Woodstock, it is more than likely that Chaucer would have spent some time in Oxford while he was employed supervising the repairs to St George's chapel at Windsor Castle.

Chaucer's granddaughter Alice, Duchess of Suffolk, lies in a fine tomb in the parish church of Ewelme in the south of the county. Thomas, Geoffrey Chaucer's son, who died in 1434, is also buried there with his wife, Matilda Burghersh. On their tomb are brass figures

Chaucer's House, Woodstock

showing Thomas in plate armour with the Chaucer unicorn at his feet, while Matilda's rest on a lion with a forked tail. Thomas, who was Member of Parliament for Oxfordshire and four times Speaker of the House of Commons, acquired the manor of Ewelme when he married Matilda.

Chaucer's works contain two main references to Oxford University.

In the *Canterbury Tales*, the Clerk of Oxenford is described in the *Prologue*:

> A Clerk there was of Oxenford also,
> That unto logick had long ygo,
> As leene was his hors as is a rake,
> And he was nat right fat, I undertake:
> But looked holwe and therto sobrely,
> Ful thredbare was his overeste courtesy:
> For he hadde geten him yet no benefice.

The Clerk did not waste either words or money, being occupied only with learning, as Chaucer puts it, 'And gladly wolde he lerne and gladly teche.'

This could never be said of Chaucer's other member of the University, Nicholas of Osney, the anti-hero of the *Miller's Tale*. As early as the twelfth century, Anglo-Norman satirists had identified a student stereotype, still apparent to this day. Nicholas, Chaucer's 'povre scholer' lodges with a carpenter, a 'riche gnof, that gestes heeld to bord,' who was evidently wealthy enough to own a sufficiently large dwelling for him to use it as a 'hostelry'. To add local colour, John the carpenter swears, by local saints, St Thomas ('of Kent' that is Thomas à Becket, the murdered Archbishop of Canterbury) who is the patron of Osney parish church. More importantly, John cries, 'Help us, seinte Frydeswyde!' invoking Frideswide, the patron saint of Oxford. He also goes off each day to work, at 'Osenay' presumably at the Abbey for there was little else there in Chaucer's day. This was in

St Thomas's parish, interestingly one of the medieval parishes which had few University connections.

Chaucer's Nicholas was by no means unusual in that he lodged with townspeople. In the early 13th century the University merely controlled the rents of lodgings and insisted that each student should be enrolled under the care of a regent master, and there its responsibility seems to have ended, with no discipline or supervision. So, in short, members of the university were not unfamiliar with townsmen (and their daughters) as lodgers, neighbours, and husbands, although obviously the Clerk of Oxenford provides an alternative view of Oxford life to that experienced by Nicholas and his kind. The Clerk has already successfully completed the BA and is well on the way to the MA, for he is reading logic.

Nicholas's landlord, the lowly carpenter, is well off, whereas Nicholas himself, although learned, is a poor scholar. He has, however, a room to himself, something which Chaucer mentions as being exceptional, indeed we know from the records of large foundations like New College that several scholars would share a chamber. To Nicholas's credit, he kept his room presentable by the use of sweet-smelling herbs. He had certainly made himself at home in the carpenter's house for he had all his astrological things around him, a cupboard in which to store his clothes and even a psaltry on which he would play and accompany himself when he sang popular songs such as *Angelus ad Virginem.*

Chaucer also describes the solidarity of Gown in the face of Town when there is an affray for, 'every clerk anon right heeld with oother,' no doubt his was aware of the St Scholastica's Day Massacre which had taken place in 1355 and which left numerous dead on both sides.

Chapter Two

John Foxe ✍ *Sir Thomas Bodley* ✍ *Sir Philip Sydney*

William Shakespeare ✍ *John Donne* ✍ *John Marston*

Robert Burton ✍ *John Milton* ✍ *John Evelyn* ✍ *Henry Vaughan*

Anthony Wood ✍ *Samuel Pepys* ✍ *John Wilmot* ✍ *John Aubrey*

John Foxe

John Foxe (1516 to 1587) was born in Boston, Lincolnshire and came up to Brasenose at the age of 16 and then was a fellow of Magdalen College from 1538 to 1545 when his strongly Protestant views led to his resignation. For while Foxe was prebend of the parish church at Shipton-under-Wychwood in West Oxfordshire he was also employed as a tutor in the home of Sir Thomas Lucy, the original for Shakespeare's Mr Justice Shallow, the 'country justice', in *The Merry Wives of Windsor.*

He moved to Europe during the reign of the Catholic Mary I but returned to England on the accession of Elizabeth I. As a writer Foxe is best remembered for his *Actes and Monuments of These Latter and Perillous Dayes* (1563). This work is usually referred to as the *Book of Martyrs* and gives a graphic account of those men and women who suffered torture and death for their Protestant beliefs. In the same year that the book appeared, Foxe was made a canon of Salisbury Cathedral.

The Oxford Martyrs, Latimer, Ridley, and Cranmer who were in fact all Cambridge men, are the best known of the 283 English

Protestant martyrs burned as heretics by order of 'Bloody' Mary Tudor in the course of her five-year reign which lasted from 1553 to 1558. These local examples went to the stake in Broad Street in 1555 and 1556.

One of the harrowing incidents related in the *Book of Martyrs* is the burning at the stake of Bishop Hooper who was burned outside his own cathedral at Gloucester while an audience watched from a gallery nearby. Archaeologists have unearthed the remains of a charred stake on the site of the memorial to Hooper which stands on the place of martyrdom.

Apparently, three attempts at lighting a suitable pyre were needed.

Here is Foxe's description of the Bishop's last moments.

'The third fire was kindled within a while after, which was more extreme than the other two. In this fire he prayed with a loud voice, 'Lord Jesus, have mercy upon me! Lord Jesus receive my spirit!' And these were the last words he was heard to utter. But when he was black in the mouth, and his tongue so swollen that he could not speak, yet his lips went until they were shrunk to the gums: and he knocked his breast with his hands until one of his arms fell off, and then knocked still with the other, while the fat, water, and blood dropped out at his fingers' ends, until by renewing the fire, his strength was gone, and his hand clave fast in knocking to the iron upon his breast. Then immediately bowing forwards, he yielded up his spirit. Thus he was three quarters of an hour or more in the fire.'

Sir Thomas Bodley

Sir Thomas Bodley (1545 to 1613) was born in Exeter in 1545 of a Protestant father who was obliged to flee the country when Mary Tudor came to the throne. Bodley was educated at Magdalen College and later, he became a Fellow of Merton. He worked as a diplomat in

several European countries before returning to England to retire. He then decided to devote the rest of his life to the restoration and refurbishment of the sadly depleted University Library which had become a victim of the religious feuds of the Reformation and Counter Reformation.

The Library was reopened in November 1602, after a lapse of some fifty years, with a stock of more than 2,000 volumes. Not only did he put all his own money and possessions, including a farm in Berkshire and land in London, into his venture, he also persuaded his many friends and colleagues to donate cash, books and manuscripts. This they did most generously.

In 1610, Bodley made an agreement with the Stationers' Company that the Library should receive a copy of each new book printed. Nowadays it is one of six such copyright libraries, along with Cambridge University Library, the National Libraries of Scotland and Wales, the British Library and that of Trinity College, Dublin. Bodley drew up plans for an eastern extension but died in January 1613 before they could come to fruition.

He died a wealthy man, having had the foresight to marry a rich widow, and his will made provision for a third floor to be added around the proposed quadrangle, now the Old Schools Quad, which initially had only two floors. Sir Thomas Bodley is buried in Merton College chapel where his monument can be found on the west wall of the ante-chapel. A modern bust of Bodley is situated on the New Bodleian Library where he supervises the comings and goings at the Old Library across Broad Street.

Left: Sir Thomas Bodley

Sir Philip Sidney

Sir Philip Sidney (1554 to 1586), a poet who was to become a soldier, was born in Penshurst, Kent. He was a member of Christ Church, and perhaps went to Cambridge, then travelled in Europe between 1572 and 1575. He incurred the wrath of Queen Elizabeth when he advised her against a proposed marriage and in 1580 left court. In 1581 Sidney became a Member of Parliament and was knighted in 1583. He was despatched to the Protestant Low Countries to help them in their struggle against Catholic Spain, but was fatally wounded at the battle of Zutphen where he spoke the often quoted words to a dying soldier, 'Thy necessity is yet greater than mine.' His literary work, written in 1578–82, was not published until after his death.

Sir Philip Sidney did not take a degree from Oxford. He did, however, have another connection with the University in that the Chancellor was none other than his Uncle Robert. This was Robert Dudley, son of the Duke of Northumberland and Earl of Leicester, who was elected Chancellor in 1564.

William Shakespeare

William Shakespeare (1564 to 1616) had a friend, John Davenant, who was the landlord of the Crown Tavern in Cornmarket. John was made Mayor in Oxford in 1622 and died in office. Shakespeare was in the habit of staying with the Davenants while in Oxford, presumably en route between London and Stratford.

The poet acted as godfather to the Davenants' son William (who was said by some to be Shakespeare's own natural child) when he was baptised in St Martin's church, Carfax, which was at that time the City Church. The body of this church was demolished at the end of the 19th century as part of a street-widening scheme, and the font by

Font in St Michael's (Shakespeare)

which Shakespeare stood sponsor can now be seen in St Michael at the North Gate, also in Cornmarket.

In later life, William Davenant took full advantage of his circumstances, claiming that Shakespeare really was his father, indeed he may well have instigated the rumour himself. Whatever the truth of the matter, he became Poet Laureate in 1638 and was knighted in 1643. Wood notes his death on 7th April 1668 and wrote 'An elegy upon the death of Sir William Davenant.'

On 23rd April, the day on which Shakespeare was born and also on which he died, a ceremony is held by the Oxford Preservation Trust. This takes place in the Painted Room at Number 3, Cornmarket, which once formed part of the Crown Tavern kept by the elder Davenant. A toast to the health of the poet is drunk in malmsey, the wine in which the unfortunate George, Duke of Clarence, is drowned in the Shakepeare play. The first time that the accompanying address was given by a woman was in 1952, when Dame Helen Gardener, then an English tutor at St Hilda's College, did the honours.

John Donne

John Donne (1572 to 1631) entered Hart Hall, the forerunner of Hertford College, in 1584 when he was only 12, and therefore too young to be forced to subscribe to the 39 Articles which professed adherence to the Protestant faith. Donne was the son of a prosperous ironmonger of Welsh ancestry, and was brought up as a Roman Catholic in London. His mother was a great niece of Sir (later Saint) Thomas More. Donne's father died when John was four, and his mother later married a physician.

After some years at Oxford (from 1584 onwards) and possibly also at Cambridge, Donne studied law at Lincoln's Inn from 1592 to 1594 and was one of the first poets to write formal verse satires in the classical mode in English.

By 1597–1598, when he became Secretary to Sir Thomas Egerton, his Catholic faith had lapsed. In 1601 he put paid to a promising career when he married Lady Egerton's niece, Ann More, in secret, and was dismissed from his position and temporarily imprisoned. For the next ten years or so, the Donne family had to be dependent on the generosity of relations and patrons.

About 1606, Thomas Morton offered Donne a benefice if he would take Anglican orders, but he was not ordained until 1615. Appointed a royal chaplain in the same year, he also received a Doctor of Divinity from Cambridge. Between 1616 and 1622 he was Reader in Divinity at Lincoln's Inn, where he preached regularly. He was devastated by the death of his wife in 1617. He preached frequently at court and in 1621 became Dean of St. Paul's Cathedral. In 1623, recovery from a life-threatening illness was the inspiration for his Devotions concerning sickness, death, and salvation. This work contains the words 'For Whom the Bell Tolls', later used by Hemingway as the title of a novel.

On March 31 1631, Donne died; his effigy, which survived the destruction of Old St. Paul's in the Great Fire of 1666, shows him in his shroud, and can be seen in the present cathedral.

John Marston

John Marston (1575 to 1634). The Brasenose College website explains how, in 1601, the name of its alumnus John Marston was linked with those of Shakespeare, Jonson and Chapman as the 'best and chiefest of our modern writers.' Marston came up to Oxford in 1592 and took his BA two years afterwards. He then went on to become a member of the Middle Temple where he had chambers from 1595 to 1606, although he was known as a poet and wit rather than a lawyer.

It is known that Marston both worked with Ben Jonson and had an ongoing literary feud with him. Marston is said to have been thrown into prison on two occasions for his offensive writing. His best known works are the plays *The Malcontent* and *The Dutch Courtesan.*

He became a man of independent means when his father died in 1599 and ten years later Marston had a complete change of occupation when he was ordained. His living from 1616 to 1631 was at Christchurch in Hampshire.

Robert Burton

Robert Burton (1577 to1640) was born in Leicestershire where he was educated at the free school in his village of Lindley and came up to Brasenose, where his elder brother was already a student, in 1593. He moved to Christ Church, where he was elected a Student (that is a Fellow) of that college in 1599, although he did not receive his BA until 1602. He took charge of the library. He spent the remainder of his life at Christ Church and was also vicar of the church of St Thomas the Martyr from 1616 until his death. A panel on the church porch has his shield; it is dated 1621, the year in which the *Anatomy of Melancholy* (subtitled What it is, With all the kinds, causes, symptomes, prognostickes, and severall cures of it), was published under the nom de plume of Democritus Junior. The work was extended and amended several times in Burton's lifetime. Its aim was to ward off Burton's own melancholy, but this was one thing in which it failed. Later writers, including Sterne, Lamb, Coleridge and Milton, made use of the book and Samuel Johnson said that the *Anatomy* was the only book which had the ability to get him out of bed two hours before he wanted to get up. It was apparently not considered bedside reading!

Burton remained unmarried and, according to his contemporary, Anthony Wood, Burton predicted the time of his own death by means of astrological calculations. Wood states that Burton hanged himself at the appointed hour on 25th January 1640 in order to make his prediction come true. There is a colourful memorial bust to Burton in Christ Church Cathedral. In the Hall he appears again in a modern glass window, dressed in black gown and skullcap.

John Milton

The ancestors of John Milton (1608 to 1674) are believed to have come from Great Milton. Milton's own father lived at Stanton St John where the poet's grandparents are buried and his father is thought to have been employed as a ranger in Shotover forest. John Milton senior, a talented musician, went to Christ Church and became a Protestant, thereby incurring his father's wrath and bringing about his being disinherited. John left Oxfordshire and went off to London where in time his son, the more famous John Milton, was born.

Although Milton himself had no direct connections with the Oxford area himself, in 1642 he married a wife who came from Forest Hill a few miles outside Oxford. She was much younger than him for he was 31 and she only 17. The wedding took place in the parish church at Forest Hill. The absorbing novel, *Wife to Mr Milton*, by Robert Graves is written from the point of view of this girl-wife, Mary Powell.

Milton must have become familiar with this part of Oxfordshire while visiting relatives and in-laws and it has been suggested that the following lines from *Il Pensiero* refer to Old Tom, the great bell at Christ Church which booms out over the city 101 times at 9.05 every evening:

> I hear the far-off curfew sound
> Over some wide-watered shore,
> Swinging slow with sullen roar.

John Evelyn

John Evelyn (1620 to 1706), the diarist and writer, was born in Wotton, Surrey. He studied at Balliol but did not take a degree, and also in London, and travelled overseas during the Civil War. During his time in Oxford, Evelyn used to patronise a gym and dancing school in Cornmarket on the site of what is now Number 35. After the Restoration he spent a lot of time at Court, sat on various committees and was a Commissioner of the Privy Seal between 1685 and 1687. From 1697 to 1703, Evelyn was treasurer of Greenwich Hospital.

His most important literary work is his *Diary*, a detailed primary source for historians of 17th-century English life. In the *Diary*, he describes, among other events, the opening of the Sheldonian Theatre on 9th July 1669. He also spent a considerable time with the members of the future Royal Society which was centred on Wadham College and his investigations included trips to the Botanic Garden where he was instructed by the Keeper, Jacob Bobart.

Henry Vaughan

The Metaphysical poet Henry Vaughan (1622 to 1695) was born in Newton-by-Usk, in South Wales. He came up to Jesus in 1638, left without taking a degree and went to London where he became a doctor; afterwards he went back to Wales where he lived near Brecon. His best-known works are the meditations *Silex scintillans* (1650) and the prose devotions *The Mount of Olives* (1652). He also published elegies, translations, and other pieces of metaphysical poetry.

Anthony Wood

The story of Anthony Wood (1632 to 1695) (or à Wood, as he later styled himself) begins with his birth in Postmasters Hall, a Merton property in Merton Street, and ends with his death in the same house. Wood is probably unique in that he spent his entire life span in the

College. Wood's autobiography spans the reigns of Charles I, the Commonwealth, Charles II, James II, and William and Mary.

Wood's first work, *History and Antiquities of Oxford*, of 1674 met with a fairly warm welcome. However, his *Athenae Oxonienses*, the first volume of which appeared in 1691, was an entirely different matter. This is an account of the City and University of Oxford and included unflattering descriptions of most of its leading members. Hardly surprisingly, it was received with protest. The second volume which appeared the following year met with an even worse reception for it was publicly burnt and its author expelled from the University.

It was not only men who met with abuse at Wood's pen. One lady is referred to as 'an imperious whore,' another a 'snotty covetous presbyterian,' while the Duchess of York is described as, 'fast and fustie; salacious; lecherous.'

Wood's comments on life in Oxford during the Civil War are very enlightening. As a youngster, he was evacuated to Thame where he stayed at the vicarage and went to the Grammar School where Hampden had been a pupil. Wood is particularly censorious of the activities of the Court of Charles I and Henrietta Maria which was at Oxford from 1642 to 1646. Contemporaries give a very different picture from that created later by romantic novelists.

In the 1660s the behaviour of the Court of Charles II, which moved to Oxford during outbreaks of plague in London, was even less admirable. Despite the courtiers being 'neat and gay in their apparell, yet they were very nasty and beastly, leaving at their departure their excrements in every corner, in chimneys, studies, colehouses, cellars. Rude, rough, whoremongers; vaine, empty, carelesse.'

Life in 17th century Oxford could be very unpleasant. Flood damage, then as now, was common and the hot, humid summers encouraged crowds of flies, although winters were much harsher. Wood notes that, in December 1679, 'A poore man died with hunger and cold: he began to die in S.Clement's parish, but the parishioners discovering it, hired or rather carried him under Magd. Tower in St

Peter's parish East to die there and so save the parish 2 or 3 shillings to burye him.' In May 1665, came hailstones as big as walnuts, or 'flat and rough like fritters, as broad as half a crowne.'

He also describes suicides, murders, and two separate instances of young girls who were to be hanged for murdering their bastard children. One was saved by being revived by the medical students who were about to anatomize her; the other was less fortunate. Under cover of darkness, the town bailiffs went to her lodgings, put her into a coffin, and hanged her from a tree as she begged the Lord to have mercy on her.

Wood and his friends also had happier and amusing things to occupy their time and minds. He tells of musical gatherings when they played the viols together in taverns, outings on the river to Medley, going to the Angel, Oxford's first coffee house in 1651, being invited to an elopement dinner at St Bartholomew's hospital off the Cowley Road, practising his 'natural genie for archaeology', and, most exciting of all for one of his temperament, exchanging insults with fellow members of the University. In 1665, the year of the great plague, a monster was 'borne at Oxon in Magd [alen] par [ish] circa 23 July having one hand, one leg, one eye in the forehead, noe nose, and its 2 eares in the nape of the neck.' Life in Oxford was seldom dull for Wood and his companions.

Wood's preoccupation, fascination almost, with health, sickness, and death, another characteristic of his century, is fascinating to the medical historian. His greatest affliction, and one which finished him off, was the painful suppression of urine. A doctor's way of telling Wood that he was beyond hope, was, that if he could not make water he must make earth, and sure enough, he was dead within the week. He died unmarried, possibly not by choice for in 1690, he complains that, 'Joan of Hedington will not have him because full of issues.' Wood is buried in the ante-chapel of Merton College chapel, at a spot which he had chosen; some reports say that he dug the grave himself, five years before he occupied it.

Anthony Wood's memorial in Merton ante-chapel

Samuel Pepys

Samuel Pepys (1633 to 1703) was a member of Magdalene College, Cambridge, which has a library named after the diarist. Despite the interaction between the two ancient universities, he does not seem to have spent much time in Oxford. In June 1668, Pepys came with his wife Elizabeth on a tour of the Oxford region for what seems to have been their first visit. The Pepys came from Huntingdon, via Buckingham and Bicester and, on arrival in Oxford, promptly embarked on a sightseeing tour. Their guide was the landlord of the inn in which they were staying. He notes, 'I out with the landlord to Brazenose College to the butteries, and in the cellar find the hand of the child of Hales – long. butler 2s.' Here Pepys apparently intended to insert the handmark's measurement, but had later forgotten it.

The couple went on to Abingdon where they heard some good music and danced and sang until it was time for supper, which cost 5 shillings. They must have stayed in Abingdon the night, for the next morning, 'up and walked to the hospitall', meaning the Long Alley almshouses which are in St Helen's churchyard. He put 2/6d into a charity box there. They returned to the inn, paid their bill, and left Oxfordshire for Hungerford by way of Wantage.

John Wilmot

John Wilmot, 2nd Earl of Rochester (1647 to 1680), was a member of Wadham College. He was the son of a prominent royalist commander who helped the future Charles II away to safety from the battlefield at Worcester and into exile. Wilmot was born at Ditchley, near Charlbury on 1st April 1647. He went to school at Burford where he proved a very able scholar, showing proficiency at Latin in particular. He went up to Wadham at the age of 12, the same year that he succeeded to the

Rochester plaque, Wadham

title and gained his MA a mere eighteen months later. At the age of 20, he was called to the House of Lords.

After leaving Oxford he set off on a 3 year Grand Tour of France and Italy and returned in time to be received at Court at Christmas 1664. Back in England, he embarked on the career which was to earn him the reputation of being the greatest libertine, prankster and wit of his day, something which put his writing ability in the shade.

Wilmot was, however, no idle courtier, for he distinguished himself in the wars against the Dutch in 1665–6. About this time he attempted to abduct an heiress, Elizabeth Malet, whom Pepys praises for her beauty, and spent a period in the Tower of London for his pains. He did marry Elizabeth and they set up house at Adderbury and produced a son and three daughters, all of whom were baptised in the parish church. As part of the 350th anniversary celebrations, a concert was held in Adderbury church and featured music from Rochester's time. Other venues for the Festival were Adderbury House, Wadham College Chapel and Bodicote and Spelsbury churches.

Affairs, juvenile pranks, drunken excesses and other disreputable behaviour followed. In Bodicote church, near Banbury, Wilmot wrote six rude lines to the parish clerk. Nevertheless, the Earl was a favourite of the King who obviously appreciated his excellent brain and appointed him Ranger of Woodstock Park which provided him with both money and a residence of his own. It was at High Lodge in what is now Blenheim Park that he did much of his writing and is said to have made his famous death-bed repentance to Gilbert Burnet. He died in the early morning of 26th July 1680, 'without any convulsion or as much as a groan.' High Lodge, where the poet is said to have died, still stands in the park at Blenheim.

After a trip out to Spelsbury church where he viewed the Wilmot vault in the north aisle, Anthony Wood noted, 'In this vault also lyes buried John earl of Rochester . . . who died in the Ranger's lodge at Woodstock parke, M. 26 July 1680 aet. 33, at two of the clock in the morning. His mother named . . . was widdow of Sir . . . Lee of Dichley. I have been credibly enformed by knowing men that this John earl of Roff. was begotten by Sir Alan Apsley, kt. This John made a great noise in the world for his noted and professed atheisme, his lampoons and other frivolous stuffe; and a greater noise after his death for his penitent departure – as may be seen in the sermon preached at his funerall . . .'

Today Wilmot is best known for his comments on Charles II, notably:

> Restless he rolls from whore to whore,
> A merry monarch, scandalous and poor.

And:

God bless our good and gracious King,
Whose promise none relies on;
Who never said a foolish thing,
Nor ever did a wise one.

Charles' response was said to have been, 'My words are my own, but my actions are my ministers.'

In the 20th century, Wilmot's true worth as a poet began to be recognised. In the programme for a 350th anniversary concert held in the Sheldonian Theatre on 25th April 1997 as part of a music festival, Mark Fisher MP wrote, 'He is a poet who goes straight into the vein. Yet his poems have struggled through a thicket of censorship and refinement for three hundred years. This Festival, I hope, will open the book and let his inconstant, insistent voice be heard.'

John Aubrey

One of the best descriptions of the antiquarian and biographer John Aubrey (1669 to 1696) was written by Aubrey himself. In his *Brief Lives,* a series of potted biographies of the notable people of his age, he writes, 'How these curiosities would be quite forgot, did not such idle fellows as I am put them down.' Nevertheless, he was the biographer of Shakespeare and was the first person to state that Stonehenge was a Druid temple. His *Lives* was published as *Brief Lives* in 1898. *Miscellanies* (1696), a work on folklore and ghost stories, was the only work to be published during his lifetime.

Aubrey was born in Easton Percy, Wiltshire, and educated at Oxford. He studied law but did not take a degree or qualify as a barrister. He became dependent on patrons, including the antiquary Elias Ashmole and the philosopher Thomas Hobbes, after being made bankrupt in 1670 by a series of lawsuits following his father's death in

1652.

Here is Aubrey on Francis Bacon: 'He had a delicate, lively, hazel eye; Dr Harvey told me it was like the eye of a viper.'

And on fellow Oxonian Walter Raleigh of Oriel: 'He took a pipe of Tobacco a little before he went to the scaffold, which some formal persons were scandalised at, but I think twas well and properly done, to settle his spirits.'

And on Thomas Hobbes who was at Hart Hall: 'His extraordinary Timourousness Mr Hobs doth very ingeniosely confess and atributes it to the influence of his Mother's Dread of the Spanish Invasion in 88, she being then with child of him.'

And on Ralph Kettell, President of Trinity, a noted disciplinarian, who used 'to go up and downe the College, and peepe in at the Keyholes to see whether the Boyes did follow their books or no.' When he discovered that one of his junior members, Ralph Bathurst, was seldom to be seen 'minding of his Booke, but mending of his old doublet or breeches,' Kettell made up his mind that this was just the sort of young man that he wanted for a son-in-law and allowed him to marry his step-daughter, a noted beauty.

John Aubrey lies in an unmarked grave somewhere in St Mary Magdalen's church in Oxford.

Chapter Three

Joseph Addison ✍ *Thomas Hearne* ✍ *Alexander Pope*

Samuel Johnson ✍ *William Shenstone* ✍ *Gilbert White*

William Mason ✍ *Oliver Goldsmith* ✍ *Edward Gibbon*

Henry James Pye

Joseph Addison

Joseph Addison (1672 to 1719) was a poet and a classicist as well as contributing to newspapers such as *The Spectator*, *The Tatler*, and *The Guardian*; he also wrote hymns.

Addison's Walk is in the grounds of Magdalen College where the writer studied law and politics. He loved to stroll along by the banks of the Cherwell as CS Lewis and his colleagues would do more than two centuries later.

When the Duke of Marlborough was at the height of his military career, many poems were written in his praise. Addison, who was at that time financially embarrassed, was commissioned by the Lord Treasurer to produce something suitable. The theme of his outpourings is the Duke's remaining calm and totally in command while the battle raged all around him. Part of it runs,

> So when an angel by divine command,
> With rising tempests shakes a guilty land,
> Such as of late o'er pale Britannia passed;

Magdalen Water Walks (Addison and CS Lewis)

Calm and serene he drives the furious blast,
And, pleased the Almighty's orders to perform,
Rides in the whirlwind, and directs the storm.

Sure enough, there are records of a violent storm which really did strike the country in November 1703. The wind was strong enough to bring down a big old walnut tree at Godstow and expose an ancient tombstone round which its roots were entangled. This stone was inscribed *Godstowe une Chauntrie* which gave rise to much discussion and conjecture concerning the person it commemorated. This storm would doubtless have still been fresh in Addison's mind when the news came through of the victory of Blenheim the following year.

Thomas Hearne

Thomas Hearne (1678–1735) was the son of the parish clerk of White Waltham in Berkshire. He came up to St Edmund Hall when he was seventeen and, like Anthony Wood at Merton, spent the rest of his life there. As an undergraduate, Hearne proved to be a very moral and studious young man and took his BA in 1699.

Already a frequenter of the Bodleian Library, he was appointed its Assistant Keeper in 1701 and promoted to Second Keeper in 1712. After a very promising start, in 1715, shortly after the accession of George I, he was 'debarr'd upon account of the oaths.' In other words, Hearne lost his position because he was a confirmed supporter of the Stuart cause and refused to take the obligatory oath of allegiance to the House of Hanover. The Library authorities went as far as having the lock changed so that Hearne might not gain admittance, so he went off to St Edmund Hall where he started to publish the work which he had been writing for several years previously.

Between 1705 and 1735 he filled 145 small notebooks with comments relevant to his position as scholar and librarian, much of the material concerning the history of the University rather in the manner of Anthony Wood the previous century. Also like Wood, Hearne made a nuisance of himself with certain influential senior members of the University; in addition, he was looked on as what might today be termed a security risk because of his anti-Hanoverian attitude. He was known as a troublemaker and in this he was a fool to himself for he was very indiscreet.

Here is Hearne on his own college:

'22nd February 1726: last Night began to be emptied Edmund Hall Bog-House, which no body I know of remembers to have been emptied. They worked but one Night, the Principal, upon consideration, ordering them to desist.'

And on George Frederick Handel who had come over to England with the Hanoverian Court:

'July 8th 1733: another Performance at 5/- a ticket, in the Theater by Mr Handel for his own benefit, continuing till about 8 o'clock. NB his book (not worth 1d.) he sells for 1s.'

and probably the most frequently quoted of all Hearne's comments, concerning the Act or conferral of degrees, in 1733:

'The Players being denied coming to Oxford by the Vice-Chancellor and that very rightly, though they might as well have been here as Handel and (his lousy Crew) a great number of forreign fidlers, they went to Abington and yesterday began to act there at which were present many Gownsmen from Oxford.'

Despite Hearne's xenophobia, an estimated 3,700 peple were said to have attended the first performance of Handel's *Athalia* in the Sheldonian Theatre.

Cox describes Hearne as a 'laborious antiquary.' Hearne became Esquire Bedel in Law in January 1715, a position which Cox himself was to hold about a century later. Hearne expected to become Printer to the University, a very prestigious post, as had his predecessors. However, the Vice-Chancellor of the day, 'chose, on his own authority, to separate the two offices, and set over the Press a common printer,' writes Cox. According to the Laudian Statutes, the Printer was to be someone well versed in Greek, Latin and philological matters who would also hold the office of Esquire Bedel in Law, rather than the other way round as would have been the case with Hearne. The result was that, 'Hearne did not long hold the staff, thus separated from the Press – he had made himself obnoxious by publishing Non-juror writings, and the Oaths of Allegiance, &c. stuck in his throat. He fell back upon the office of Under-Librarian at the Bodleian; but even there, his politics were turned against him. On being deprived of that post, he retired to a studious life in St Edmund Hall.' He wrote many books on antiquities and toured round the country noting down all that he saw.

Although he was satirised by Pope as 'Wormius, dry as dust,' Hearne is still very readable. It is those prejudices and indiscretions that brought about his downfall that make Hearne such a valuable source of information for students of everyday life in 18th-century England, for he hides nothing whether he is writing of events of world importance or the minutiae of college life. He made a living by his own writing efforts and, after he died on 20th June 1735, more than £1000 was found in his room.

Alexander Pope

Alexander Pope (1688 to 1744) was born into a Roman Catholic London family. In 1700, the family moved to Binfield, Berkshire. Because he was a Catholic, Pope was unable to attend university, for in his day Oxford and Cambridge were open only to members of the Anglican Church. In addition, he had asthma and tuberculosis with a curvature of the spine which meant that he failed to reach more than 4'6" in height. His poems were satirical and he was frequently engaged in feuds with fellow writers. His best results were in the field of the heroic couplet, in particular *The Rape of the Lock* which he produced between1712 and 1714.

He set about translating Homer's *Illiad* in 1715, a task which was to take him five years. The medieval Pope's Tower at Stanton Harcourt got its name from the fact that Pope stayed there in the summers of 1717 and 1718, busy with his translation. This occupancy is marked by scratch marks on a pane of glass which read, 'In the year 1718 Alexander Pope finish'd here the fifth volume of Homer.' The piece of red glass was afterwards taken off to the Harcourt family's other estate at Nuneham Courtenay.

What we now call Pope's Tower is a three-storied structure, the ground floor of which has a private chapel with a fan-vaulted roof. The building was used as the quarters of the Harcourt's family chaplain during the Middle Ages. There is a room above the chapel and up a winding staircase is the panelled study which gave the poet views towards the spires of Oxford if he ventured out onto the leads. These rooms were also occupied by the children of Rajah Brooke of Sarawak who rented them for a holiday home.

In his tower, Pope was free to work away in perfect solitude broken only by visits from his friend John Gay. On the back of a letter addressed to Pope which was written to let Pope know that Gay had died, Swift, who was sorting Pope's papers, discovered that the poet had written, 'On my dear friend, Mr Gay's death. Received December 15th; but not read till the 20th, by an impulse foreboding some misfortune.' Pope wrote a long and emotional epitaph for his friend.

Apart from his translating work, Pope wrote letters and among his correspondents was Lady Mary Wortley Montague. In one letter, he mentions the local tragedy of John Hewett and Sarah Drew, an engaged couple who were struck by lightning while sheltering under a tree. That very morning, John had obtained her father's permission to marry his sweetheart. There was, writes Pope, 'so loud a crack, as if the heavens had burst asunder.' When their neighbours went to look for the couple, 'They saw a little smoke, and after, this faithful pair – John with one arm about his Sarah's neck, and the other held over her face, as if to screen her from the lightning. They were dead!' he adds somewhat unnecessarily. They were buried the next day in the same grave and Lord Harcourt, at Pope's request, put up a monument to their memory. Naturally, the poet wrote an epitaph for John and Sarah as well.

In the parish church of Stanton Harcourt there is an epitaph to Lord Harcourt's only son written by Pope, as well as one by Congreve. Yet another of Pope's epitaphs is in Christ Church Cathedral where he wrote of Bishop Berkeley who died in 1753, 'To Berkeley Ev'ry Virtue under Heav'n.'

Pope was familiar with other parts of Oxfordshire. He was a frequent visitor to Mapledurham House, to the south of the county, where he went to stay with his friends Theresa and Martha Blount;

Charles Jervas's portraits of all three of them are kept in the house. Martha was the poet's favourite and the 'scornful beauty' with 'the brightest eyes of Britain,' as he describes her. When she came down from the social whirl of London to the seclusion of Oxfordshire:

> She went to plain-work, and to purling brooks,
> Old fashioned halls, dull aunts, and croaking rooks,
> She went from opera, park, assembly, play,
> To morning walks, and prayers three times a day.

Rosy-red Mapledurham House, an Elizabethan mansion on the banks of the Thames, was built by Sir Michael Blount in 1588, the year of the Spanish Armada. It is still occupied by descendants of the Blount family. In the interior are paintings and family portraits dating back to the 16th century and a Strawberry Hill gothick family chapel. Mapledurham parish church has a Roman Catholic south aisle which remains in the ownership of the Blount family; their religious persuasion was something they had in common with Pope.

Martha Blount kept up a lively correspondence with Pope but would not go to visit him when he was dying. Nevertheless, he left his books, silver plate and a thousand pounds to her.

And here are Pope's lines about Blenheim Palace, entitled *Upon the Duke of Marlborough's House at Woodstock*:

> 'Thanks, sir,' cried I, ''tis very fine,
> But where d'ye sleep, or where d'ye dine?
> I find by all you have been telling,
> That 'tis a house, but not a dwelling.'

It was he who wrote the often-quoted couplet:

> Lie heavy on him, earth, for he
> Laid many a heavy weight on thee,

in relation to Sir John Vanburgh who had designed the Palace.

Pope stayed at Tusmore, then the seat of the Fermors, one of whom was his friend Arabella, the heroine of the *Rape of the Lock,* and he also paid visits to Rousham in the north of the county, where the owners, the Cottrell-Dormer family, played host to John Gay and Horace Walpole. When visiting the Duke of Argyll at Adderbury, Pope would have stayed at the house once owned by John Wilmot, Earl of Rochester; here he penned some somewhat sycophantic verses contrasting the Duke's virtues with that Earl's well known vices.

Samuel Johnson

Samuel Johnson (1709 to 1784). The lexicographer, critic and poet was born in Lichfield, Staffordshire, the son of a bookseller. He was at Pembroke College, where, in 1728, he had rooms on the second floor above the gatehouse. Johnson had been admitted to the University as a servitor, that is a student who kept himself at university by doing menial tasks for other students. He was fined for not attending lectures or tutorials and complained 'Sir, you have sconced me two pence for a lecture not worth a penny.' Johnson left Pembroke before taking a degree and became a teacher.

Johnson said of his college, 'Sir, we are a nest of singing birds'. Pembroke treasures a desk and an enormous teapot which belonged to Johnson, as well as his portrait by Reynolds. They form part of a collection of Johnsoniana housed in the college library.

In 1737 Johnson went to London, and worked as a journalist. From 1747 onwards Johnson spent eight years working on his *Dictionary of the English Language.* He held back the publication of the dictionary until he could add the honorary Master of Arts degree which he

Right: Dr Johnson's desk, Pembroke

received from the University in 1775 to his name on the title page. He started the periodical, *The Rambler,* in 1750. In 1762, he was given a crown pension, which enabled him to launch himself into polite society, notably in the Literary Club, of which he was a founder member (1764). The following year he produced his edition of Shakespeare and in 1772 occupied himself with political pamphleteering. The account of his tour of Scotland embarked on with Boswell in 1773, makes enlightening and entertaining reading; he later wrote *Lives of the Poets* between 1779 and 1781.

In the August of 1754, Johnson walked over from Oxford to Elsfield to visit the Radcliffe librarian and Anglo-Saxon scholar, Wise, at his house there. On this occasion Johnson was accompanied by his friend Thomas Warton, President of Trinity and editor of the literary miscellany entitled the *Oxford Sausage.* Warton (who came up to Trinity as a lad of 16, became a Fellow of the College, died in its Senior Common Room and is buried in the ante-chapel), also went with him on a country ramble which included visits to the ruins of Osney and Rewley abbeys, on the western outskirts of Oxford. After a good half-hour's silent meditation, Johnson is reported to have announced, 'I viewed them with indignation!'

Johnson and Boswell stayed at the Red Lion at Henley-on-Thames on 21st March 1776. Boswell notes, 'We happened to lie this night at the inn at Henley where Shenstone wrote these lines.' In 1738 William Shenstone had scratched with a diamond on a windowpane:

> Who e'er has travelled life's dull round
> Where e'er his stages may have been,
> May sigh to think he still has found
> The warmest welcome at an inn.

In June 1784 shortly before his death, Johnson, accompanied by the faithful Boswell, drove out from Oxford to have dinner with William Julius Mickle who lived near the Crown Inn at Wheatley. Mickle was a Scot who came to Oxford to work as a printer. Like John Milton, he married a girl called Mary from Forest Hill. Mickle died on a visit to Forest Hill and was buried there in 1788, on the north side of the churchyard, under a tombstone which reads,

'Mickle who bade the strong poetic tide
Roll o'er Britannia's shores in Lusitanian pride'

Boswell and Johnson also went out to Iffley to dine with the Principal of St Mary Hall, Dr Nowell, 'at his beautiful villa at Iffley, on the banks of the Isis.'

It was while he was staying at Oxford on that occasion that Johnson heard that his dear friend, Mrs Thrale, had decided to marry Signor Piozzi; this unwelcome news is thought to have hastened his death.

William Shenstone

William Shenstone (1714 to 1763) was born in Halesowen, at that time in Worcestershire, and grew up to be an avid reader as Johnson's *Preface to Shenstone* relates. He went to a dame school, then to the local grammar school and afterwards had tuition from 'an eminent school-master at Solihul.'

In 1732 Shenstone went up to Johnson's college, Pembroke, which the latter notes as, 'a society which for half a century has been eminent for English poetry and elegant literature. Here it appears that he found delight and advantage; for he continued his name in the book ten years, though he took no degree.' While he was up at Oxford he wrote poetry and published a small collection anonymously. Most of Shenstone's work is of the classical variety and his best known lines are probably those which he scratched on the window pane at Henley in 1758.

Gilbert White

Gilbert White (1720 to 1793), clergyman and naturalist, was born in Selborne, Hampshire. He was elected a Fellow of Oriel in 1744, was ordained in 1751 and became a Proctor for the following year.

White returned to his native parish and from 1755 lived there as curate, keeping a journal in which he recorded many observations about his garden, the plants and animal life in the vicinity of Selborne, of which one of the stars was an elderly tortoise named Timothy. White's letters, which cover 20 years, were published as *The Natural History and Antiquities of Selborne* in 1789. Now an English classic as well as a naturalist's handbook, it has the distinction of never having been out of print.

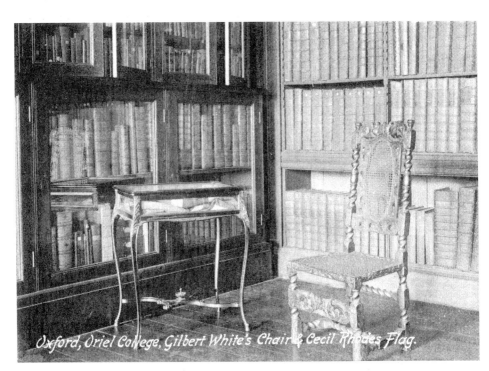

Oxford, Oriel College, Gilbert White's Chair & Cecil Rhodes Flag.

Oriel, Gilbert White's chair

William Mason

William Mason (1725 to 1797) was a poet who assisted Capability Brown in the landscaping of the grounds of Nuneham Park at Nuneham Courtenay when the old village was removed from the Park and its cottages repositioned along the main road.

He was a graduate of St John's College, Cambridge and his surroundings there may have generated his interest in landscape gardening. He was also a very competent musician and held the post of Precentor at York Minster for 32 years.

Mason was popular in his own age, his poem *Isis* being well known at one time, but his work was little read afterwards. He supported the Americans in their bid for independence but lived to modify his republican sympathies after the atrocities of the French Revolution. His poem *Isis* appeared as a protest against the Jacobitism which was supposed to be rife in Oxford and was countered by Warton's *Triumph of Isis*. More successful was Mason's descriptive poem, *English Garden,* which first appeared in 1772 and brought its writer some renown.

At his death, a memorial to Mason was placed in Poet's Corner in Westminster Abbey.

Oliver Goldsmith

Irishman Oliver Goldsmith (1728 to 1774) was not an Oxford graduate, neither did he live in the city. As regards education, however, to an Oxbridge man he would have been considered the next best thing, for he went to the Anglo-Irish Trinity College, Dublin, which has close associations with Oxford. Afterwards Goldsmith went to Edinburgh University, where he studied medicine for two years.

His works include the novel *The Vicar of Wakefield* (1766), which became one of the most popular works of fiction in English and the humorous play *She Stoops to Conquer* (1773). In 1761, Goldsmith met Samuel Johnson; the two men became friends and it was Johnson who managed to arrange for *The Vicar of Wakefield* to be published. Its success saved Goldsmith from being thrown into a debtors' prison because he was unable to pay for his lodgings.

Goldsmith's other works include the poem *The Deserted Village* (1770), which forms his connection with Oxfordshire. Although the village is called Auburn in the poem, it is believed that the poet was inspired to write it by the case of Nuneham Courtenay. This early example of planned development, which straddles the A423, was conceived when the first Earl Harcourt built his new mansion in Nuneham Park in the 1760s. Harcourt's dislike of the existing view, which included his tenants' various cottages and hovels, prompted him to re-locate the entire peasantry into state-of-the-art accommodation at a discreet distance from Nuneham House.

Apart from a restaurant (which was once the Harcourt Arms public house) and a garage, Nuneham consists of semi-detached red brick cottages complete with wooden shutters, among which are a post office and a village shop. All Saints chapel stands in the park; dating from 1764, it was designed by the Earl himself. A second All Saints, 1872/4, acts as the church for the village.

House and park were acquired by Oxford University for use as a conference centre and bookstore for the Bodleian Library. In the park is the Harcourt Aboretum, part of the University and famous for its peacocks, rhododendrons and carpets of bluebells in the spring. Nearer the river is the ornate stone conduit which was brought to Nuneham in 1787 from Carfax in Oxford.

In retrospect, Goldsmith's indignation at the removal of the villagers from park to highway would seem to be unjustified, for today their new quarters are still very desirable residences and continue to fetch high prices whenever they come on the market.

Edward Gibbon

Edward Gibbon (1737 to 1794) was born at Putney, near London, and grew into a sickly child. He was not expected to reach adulthood and he relates how his parents baptised all their successive sons Edward as well, as if they expected that he would not live long enough to continue the family Christian name. Fortunately for English literature, the elder Gibbons were mistaken and it was Edward's younger siblings who died in infancy.

He was sent off to Westminster School which proved to be unsuitable to one of his temperament. Schooldays were certainly not the happiest days of his life. Edward did, however, greatly enjoy reading and he developed an interest in Roman history. This was to result in *The History of the Decline and Fall of the Roman Empire,* the work for which he is best remembered; this appeared between 1776 and 1778 and was to become controversial on account of its criticism of Christianity.

A few days before his 15th birthday, Gibbon was sent up to Magdalen College as a gentleman-commoner. If Westminster School had failed to please him, Oxford turned out to be an even worse experience. Scholarship, he found, was practically non-existent and the Anglican Church left much to be desired. The teenage Gibbon was left to his own devices and, like many gifted scholars who were to come after him, he became a Roman Catholic. This was on 8th June 1753, and that same month, still only 16 years of age, he left Oxford after spending only one year there. This he referred to as the most idle and unprofitable of his entire life.

Gibbon's opinion of Oxford in his day is supported by both the writings of his contemporaries and the findings of later historians. Despite his failing to complete his university education, Gibbon was to make an enormous contribution to scholarship, influencing future generations of writers and historians, among whom is classicist and crime writer Colin Dexter (qv).

Henry James Pye

Henry James Pye (1745 to 1813) of Faringdon House was educated at Magdalen College where he took his BA in 1763. Pye was an MP 1784 to 1790, and also a magistrate. He published many volumes of verse and was, for some inexplicable reason, created Poet Laureate to George III, a position which he held from 1790 to 1813. It has been suggested that this was a reward for his support of William Pitt the Younger in the House of Commons. The king apparently regretted the choice, however, for he was heard to exclaim 'what what, not more Pye!' ; the poet was most prolific.

The appointment was considered ludicrous, and his birthday odes to George III were a particular source of ridicule. His first official effort referred to 'vocal groves and feathered choir' and caused the editor of the *Shakespearean,* George Steevens, to say:

> And when PYE was opened the birds began to sing;
> Was not that a dainty dish to set before the king?

This piece of satirical verse was later turned into the nursery rhyme:

> Sing a song of sixpence,
> A pocket full of rye;
> Four and twenty blackbirds baked in a pie.
> When the pie was opened,
> The birds began to sing;
> Was not that a dainty dish
> To set before the king?

The Poet Laureate's most ambitious poem was the epic *Alfred* which he produced in 1801; not only were Pye's poems numerous, they were sufficiently dreadful for Sir Walter Scott to describe them as 'contemptible.'

Pye took the opportunity of committing to verse the ascent of James Sadler, pastry cook of the parish of St Peter in the East in Oxford and our earliest aeronaut. Sadler constructed his own hot air balloon and, after several successful trips, took his patron, the politician William Windham, up with him over Surrey. It was Windham's fame, rather than Sadler's achievement, which stimulated Pye's interest in the flight.

Pye was obviously more at home with his *Summary of the Duties of a Justice of the Peace Out of Sessions* (1808), which drew on his own magisterial experience.

Faringdon House, in the Market Place, was built by Henry Pye to replace the house which was held for the King by Sir Robert Pye during the Civil War. It was bombarded by his son, who was on the Presbyterian side, but somehow managed to inflict little damage. Today, the four-and-twenty blackbirds can be seen, still singing away, in a giant terracotta pie over the doorway to the house.

Chapter Four

William Wordsworth ✍ *Robert Southey* ✍ *Jane Austen*

Walter Savage Landor ✍ *Percy Bysshe Shelley* ✍ *John Keats*

William Wordsworth

William.Wordsworth (1770 to 1850) was a Cambridge graduate who was fascinated by Oxford High Street, the curves of which he described as 'stream-like windings.' In *From Oxford, May 30th, 1820,* he writes:

> I slight my own beloved Cam, to range
> Where silver Isis leads my stripling feet;
> Pace the long avenue, or glide adown
> The stream-like wanderings of that glorious street –
> An eager Novice robed in fluttering gown!

He also ventured further afield into the county. In *On a Parsonage in Oxfordshire,* he writes about Souldern, a village where Wordsworth used to visit Robert Jones, a friend from Cambridge, who was the incumbent.

> Where holy ground begins, unhallowed end,
> Is marked by no distinguishable line;
> The turf unites, the pathways intertwine;
> And wheresoe'er the stealing footstep tends,

High Street in the 19th century (Wordsworth)

Garden and Domain where kindred, friends,
And neighbours rest together, here confound
There several features, mingled like the sound
Of many waters, or as evening blends
With shady night. Soft airs, from shrub and flower,
Waft fragrant greetings to each silent grave;
And while those lofty poplars gently wave
Their tops, between them comes and goes a sky
Bright as the glimpses of eternity,
To saints accorded in their mortal hour.

A parsonage has since replaced the old rectory at Souldern.

On 12th June 1839, an honorary Doctorate of Civil Law was conferred on Wordsworth. Cox describes the scene in the Theatre, 'his reception was overpowering to others, though he stood it firm and *apparently* unmoved as one of his Westmoreland mountains. Keble, as

Professor of Poetry, did him ample honour from the Rostrum. I was honoured by a call from 'the philosophic poet,' who was brought to my house by a friend to hear his little poem, 'She dwelt among the untrodden ways,' sung as it had been admirably set to music by Professor Donkin. Wordsworth remarked with regret that one stanza (which he directly repeated) had been omitted.'

Robert Southey

The poet Robert Southey (1774 to1843) was born in Bristol and went to Westminster School. Like Shelley, Southey was influenced by the radical opinions of the age and he too wrote a pamphlet which led to his being expelled. When the time came for him to go to Oxford he was refused admission to Christ Church despite, or maybe because of, its connections with Westminster School. This was a disappointment to Southey's family, but he made the best of the situation and went to Balliol instead.

Once at Oxford, however, Southey found his studies less than stimulating and looked around for outside interests. His family tried to persuade him to enter the Church, but this he resisted. In the autumn of 1793, he left Oxford for a period. Partly to finance his intended marriage to Edith Fricker but also to avoid becoming a clergyman, Southey toyed with the idea of taking up medicine as a career, but on his return to Oxford he complained that he had an 'aversion to the dissecting room.' He left Oxford after only two terms.

In 1813, he became Poet Laureate, after Scott had refused the position. He was an early admirer of the French Revolution, as is shown by his epic poem *Joan of Arc* (1796), but later gave up his revolutionary ideals, and from 1808 was a regular contributor to the *Tory Quarterly Review*. In *The Doctor* (1834–47), a collection of anecdotes, Southey included the well-known children's tale of 'The

Three Bears'. In 1835, He turned down both the editorship of *The Times* and a baronetcy.

Southey was evidently moved by the sight of the Martyrs' Memorial and penned *For a monument at Oxford*:

> Latimer and Ridley in the flames
> Bore witness to the truth. If thou hast walk'd
> Uprightly through the world, proud thoughts of joy
> Will fill thy breast in contemplating here
> Congenial virtue. But if thou hast swerved
> From the right path, if thou hast sold thy soul,
> And served, with hireling and apostate zeal,
> The cause thy heart disowns, – oh! cherish well
> The honourable shame that sure this place
> Will wake within thee, timely penitent,
> And let the future expiate the past.

GV Cox probably does indeed speak for most members of the University when he writes, of November 1839, 'it was right and reasonable that our Alma Mater (the great majority of whose sons were in this, as in many former trials, true to their Church of England principles) should wish to show that she had not been influenced by the cloud [that is the Tractarian, or Oxford, Movement] that had hung over her. This healthy feeling found its expression in the erection of the beautiful cross and monument to the memory of Cranmer, Ridley, and Latimer. It was a noble proof (though a somewhat tardy one) that Oxford still cherished the memory of those great martyrs to the Reformation. The subscription was a very great one (£5000), and was raised with wonderful rapidity; out of it, besides the Martyrs' Memorial, was also built an additional aisle on the north side of [St Mary] Magdalen parish church – to be called the Martyrs' Aisle. It had been found impracticable to get a site in Broad Street, the actual scene of the martyrdom.'

Jane Austen

The usually genteel and tactful Jane Austen (1775 to 1817) was certainly no admirer of Oxford. In the spring of 1783 when she was seven, she went there with her ten-year-old sister, Cassandra and their cousin Jane Cooper aged twelve. During their stay, which was to be taught by a Mrs Cawley, the Austen girls had a brother, James, who was at St John's College. The Oxford connection was strengthened by the fact that Mrs Austen's uncle was Theophilus Leigh, Master of Balliol.

This Mrs Cawley was the widow of Ralph Cawley, Principal of Brasenose from 1770 to 1777. She had lived in the Principal's Lodgings in the Old Quadrangle overlooking Radcliffe Square until they moved to their new lodgings on the High Street in 1771. When she was widowed, Mrs Cawley would have been obliged to move elsewhere.

Jane is supposed to have complained, 'I never was but once at Oxford in my life and I am sure I never wish to go there again. They dragged me through so many dismal chapels, dusty libraries and greasy halls that it gave me the vapours for two days afterwards.'

Walter Savage Landor

Walter Savage Landor (1775 to 1864) was born in Warwick. He was sent down from both Rugby School and Trinity College, in the latter case for firing a gun at the window of a fellow student who happened to be a Tory and had the bad luck to live opposite him in the quad. To make matters worse, Landor refused to own up to the attack. Despite his being sent down and his difficult character, he became an outstanding classicist. He published *Poems* in 1795, *Examination of Shakespeare* (1834), and *Hellenics* (1847). His best-known work is the prose dialogue *Imaginary Conversations* (1824– 9). Landor's long life was punctuated by quarrels and outbursts of temper, but ironically, one of his most famous lines is, 'I strove with none, for none was worthy of my strife.' Landor was fortunate in having as a friend the poet Robert Browning who assured him a more comfortable old age than might have been expected from his life style. Landor is buried near Elizabeth Barrett Browning in the Protestant cemetery in Florence.

Percy Bysshe Shelley

Percy Bysshe Shelley (1792 to 1822) was born in 1792 at Field Place near Horsham, Sussex, the eldest son of a wealthy country squire. The young Shelley felt persecuted by his down-to-earth father, and this may have triggered off the attitude which earned him the nickname 'Mad Shelley' while he was at Eton in the years from 1804 to 1810. During his only year at University College (1810–1811), Shelley, supported by a college friend Thomas Jefferson Hogg, published a pamphlet called *The Necessity of Atheism*. This 'atheism' was an expression of their discontent with all aspects of the Establishment. This sentiment became *de rigeur* in the 1960s, but unfortunately for Shelley and Hogg, they were far ahead of their time. The fact that Shelley refused to admit authorship, compounded their offence and the result was that both were sent down from the University. Far from bringing Shelley to his senses, however, his expulsion served to fan the flames of his rebellious nature, a personality trait that was to stay with him for the remainder of his short life which was full of attempts at political reform and concern for the rights of the individual.

Nevertheless, throughout his Oxford year Shelley made the most of everything it had to offer: chemical experiments in his rooms, poetic wanderings around the Oxfordshire countryside, reading and writing poetry and practising pistol shooting. Shelley must have enjoyed something of his short stay at Oxford, if it was only the uncluttered aspect of the surrounding countryside in those pre-enclosure times. He wrote, 'The country near Oxford has no pretensions to peculiar beauty, but it is quiet, and pleasant, and rural, and purely agricultural after the good old fashion; it is not only unpolluted by manufactures and commerce, but is exempt from the desecration of modern husbandry, of a system which accounts the farmer a manufacturer of hay and corn: I delight to wander over it.' Shelley's opinion was shared by his friend Hogg who was particularly fond of walking on Shotover and also by the reactionary Scott, but certainly not by the agriculturalist Arthur Young who could appreciate the potential benefits of enclosure.

On July 8, 1822, Shelley drowned in the Gulf of Spezia near Lerici in Italy. His memorial, erected by the college in 1894, was originally

University College, Shelley Memorial

destined for the British Cemetery in Rome where Shelley is buried, but was refused by the authorities there. By Onslow Ford, it stands in a sort of domed mausoleum where a weeping muse guards the poet's dead body. The figure is rounded and rather effeminate, particularly when viewed from the rear, which gives rise to the speculation that its model was a girl. It has been tampered with by generations of undergraduate vandals and traces of their attentions are faintly visible in the remaining specks of orange paint. It was this disfigurement which prompted the Ashmolean to follow the example of the British Cemetery when asked by University College to accept the figure when the college wished to build on the site of the Memorial. The site is important as it is where a house once stood in which Robert Boyle perfected the air-pump in 1659 and demonstrated how air might be compressed, so opening up the way for the invention of the pneumatic tyre.

John Keats

John Keats (1795 to 1821) was one of Oxford's greatest admirers, believing it to be the loveliest city in the world. Keats had no personal connections with the place, being apprenticed to a London surgeon and then becoming a medical student. Like several other medical men, Keats also turned his attentions to writing and in 1814 gave up any ideas of becoming a doctor.

Through a mutual friend, he met Benjamin Bailey, an undergraduate reading Theology at Magdalen Hall. Bailey was very interested in poetry, his favourites being Milton and Wordsworth and this forged a bond between the two young men. In the summer of 1817, Keats spent the last few weeks of the Long Vacation at Magdalen Hall at Bailey's invitation. The letters which Keats wrote to his friends from Oxford show that he enjoyed his stay in and around the city and that he and

Bailey made trips out and about, notably to Stratford-upon-Avon. Particularly valuable are those to his sister Fanny in which he describes Oxford and tells her about his work, including the story of Endymion.

Keats must have spent some time wandering through the streets and lanes of Oxford, for he notes that its streams and rivulets were 'more in number than your eyelashes.' He also wrote what is arguably one of the worst examples of his verse:

> The Gothic looks solemn,
> The plain Doric column
> Supports an old Bishop and Crozier,
> The mouldering arch,
> Shaded o'er by a larch
> Stands next door to Wilson the Hosier.

Keats developed tuberculosis in 1818 and in an attempt to combat the disease he went to Italy, where he had a brief respite before he collapsed and died in Rome in 1821. He is buried in the Protestant Cemetery there.

Chapter Five

John Henry Newman ✍ Alfred, Lord Tennyson ✍ John Ruskin

Richard Francis Burton ✍ Matthew Arnold ✍ Thomas Hughes

R D Blackmore ✍ Edward Bradley ✍ Charles Lutwidge Dodgson

William Morris ✍ Algernon Swinburne ✍ Walter Pater

Thomas Hardy ✍ Andrew Lang ✍ GM Hopkins

John Henry Newman

John Henry Newman (1801 to 1890) is more often thought of as a theologian than as a literary giant and the Oxford, or Tractarian, Movement will always be associated with him. When the time came for Newman to be sent off to university, his father had difficulty making up his mind whether to send him to Oxford or Cambridge, for in those days application was a much more personal and informal business than it is today. With the carriage at the very door, Newman Senior was only decided by a friend who advised sending John to Exeter College. However, there were no vacancies at Exeter, so he crossed over Broad Street to Trinity and matriculated at that college, even though he had himself never heard of it. If Newman had gone to Cambridge, perhaps there would have been a Cambridge Movement instead of an Oxford one, or he might have just stayed in the Anglican Church.

After a successful period at Trinity and having been elected a Fellow of Oriel in 1822, Newman began to preach the famous sermons in the

1801 –1890

John H. (and. Newman

JH Newman

University church which drew instant attention and attracted many listeners 'which with their nobility of spirit touched the hearts of many who could not accept their dogmatic appeal. But it was not until Keble preached his stirring sermon on National Apostasy in 1833 that the new crusade began' says the *Oxford University Handbook.* The University, as a pillar of the Established Church, felt itself under threat and battle lines were drawn. Oxford was divided internally. The discussions and debates raged on, the result of the crisis of 1845 being the loss of several of the University's leading men who left the Church of England to become Roman Catholics. These included John Henry Newman.

Newman's first novel, *Loss and Gain* (subtitled *the Story of a Convert*), appeared in 1848. According to the back cover of the OUP World's Classics edition, it is the story of a young man's 'search for faith and certainty amid the competing loyalties of early Victorian Oxford.'

Newman was curate of St Clement's and Vice Principal of St Alban's Hall. After he had been appointed Vicar of St Mary the Virgin in 1828, he discovered that the hamlet of Littlemore (which lay within the parish, although some three miles away), had neither church nor chapel. Intending to hold a weekly service and give catechism classes there, Newman started off by hiring a room for the purpose. He also rented accommodation for himself in a cottage which belonged to a Mrs Barnes. Then he began the task of collecting sufficient money to build a church at Littlemore.

In April 1835 Oriel College donated a site and the foundation stone for the church was laid on 21st July by Newman's mother who lived nearby with his sisters at Iffley. The nave of the new church of St Mary and St Nicholas was consecrated by the Bishop of Oxford on 22nd September the following year. It was later extended (although its maximum seating capacity is still only 150) and accorded the status of an independent parish.

Next, Newman bought up a range of stables which he had converted into a college. In 1841 he moved into the parsonage which formed part of these premises; it was here, in October 1845, that he was to be received into the Church of Rome. *Punch* referred to Newman's Oxford as being 'The Half-Way House to Rome.'

Newman's church today describes itself on its website as 'modern catholic,' adding that 'though as a genuine parish church many of the congregation could be described as central Anglican.'

Alfred, Lord Tennyson

Alfred, Lord Tennyson (1809 to 1892) was born at Somersby in Lincolnshire, the fourth of twelve children and was taught at home by his father until 1827 when he went up to Cambridge where, in 1829, he both met his great friend Arthur Henry Hallam and won the Chancellor's Prize Medal for his poem *Timbuctoo*. Two years later, tragedy struck when his father died and Tennyson was forced to leave Cambridge.

In 1836, Tennyson began his courtship of Emily Sellwood, but it was not until 14 years later that he married her at Shiplake on one of the loveliest stretches of the Thames. Like the poet, Emily came from Lincolnshire. She was the daughter of a lawyer and Tennyson met her at Somersby Rectory when she was only 17. Six years later Emily was bridesmaid when Tennyson's brother married her sister. The couple were instantly attracted to each other, but marriage was out of the question because of Tennyson's impoverished state. In 1850, when *In Memoriam,* which had been written in memory of Arthur Hallam, proved so successful, they were able to marry after 14 years of courtship. They had their furniture given to them and Tennyson had a bank loan of £300 and the promise of a yearly royalty from the poem. On the day of the long awaited wedding, the dresses and the cake were late arriving; nevertheless Tennyson claimed that it was the nicest wedding that he had ever been to. Afterwards, the newly weds set up home in Sussex.

The following year their first child was stillborn, but 1852 saw the birth of their son, Hallam Tennyson, who was to become the second Lord Tennyson and be awarded an honorary DCL at Viscount Goschen's installation in 1904.

John Ruskin

John Ruskin (1819 to 1900) was born in London and came up to Christ Church where he took a Fourth in Classics and a Fourth in Maths in 1842. When Ruskin arrived at Oxford in 1837, his mother, anxious because this was his first time away from home, took lodgings at 90 High Street where she would summon him to take tea with her every day. Despite such maternal distractions, Ruskin won the Prize for English verse in 1839 with *Salsette and Elephanta.*

After graduating, he met JMW Turner, whose work he defended in his work *Modern Painters* (1843–60). He was also a friend and supporter of the Pre-Raphaelites and of the architects involved in the Gothic Revival. Ruskin was not, however, indiscriminate in his admiration for artists, as his comment on Whistler's *Nocturne in Black and Gold* shows, for he said 'Never expected to hear a coxcomb ask two hundred guineas for flinging a pot of paint in the public's face.'

The five volumes of *Modern Painters*, along with *The Seven Lamps of Architecture* (1848) and *The Stones of Venice* (1851–3), made Ruskin into a sort of guru and *Unto This Last* (1860) is said to have influenced Gandhi. One statement which must have appealed to him is 'Whereas it has long been known and declared that the poor have no right to the property of the rich, I wish it also to be known and declared that the rich have no right to the property of the poor.'

Ruskin's concerns about what was going on around him went far deeper than matters of art and architecture and encompassed a desire to improve social and moral trends. Like Matthew Arnold, he condemned the ever-increasing materialism of his time and campaigned for a return to former values by which the labourer was worthy of his hire.

He did not confine himself to writing and lecturing but turned his energies to becoming involved in the provision of education and adequate housing for workers. In *Time and Tide* he wrote 'To make your children capable of honesty is the beginning of education.'

In 1848 he married Euphemia Chalmers Gray. The union proved disastrous for Ruskin was an idealist. It was rumoured that he refused to consummate the marriage because his wife had neglected to inform him of a mole somewhere on her person, which Ruskin found out about after the ceremony. Whether this is true or not, in 1855 Euphemia was granted a decree of nullity. Ruskin did not defend the action and she married the Pre-Raphaelite artist John Millais.

On the death of his father in 1864, he became a wealthy man and used much of this money to help artists establish themselves and towards a housing campaign.

Ruskin became the first Slade Professor of Fine Art at Oxford in 1870, shortly before moving to the Lake District, and he occupied the Chair until 1879. He again occupied the Chair from 1883 to 1885 and was a great advocate of university education for women. His last work was an unfinished autobiography, *Praeterita*. Always something of an eccentric, Ruskin suffered a series of mental breakdowns; nevertheless,

University Museum (John Ruskin and CL Dodgson)

he received an honorary DCL from the University in 1893.

Apart from a plaque, little trace is left of the work done by a gang of student labourers who attempted some road building in North Hinksey where a plaque commemorates their efforts. Perhaps the most noteworthy aspect of this scheme is the fact that Ruskin managed to persuade Oscar Wilde to join in. 'Even digging, rightly done, is an art,' he assured them.

Unfortunately, the builders of the University Museum of Natural History were unimpressed with such amateur enthusiasm and felt compelled to redo the attempts at carving which Ruskin had made in the building. Surviving memorials are the School of Drawing and Fine Art which adjoins the Examination Schools in High Street and the College in Walton Place, both of which bear his name.

Richard Francis Burton

Richard Francis Burton (1821 to 1890) was a member of Trinity College but was rusticated, that is temporarily expelled, from Trinity for being rude and generally uncooperative, his major offence being to challenge a fellow student to a duel. He joined the army and never came back to Oxford. Instead, he went to India and became an explorer as far afield as the Middle East and Africa. Between 1853 and 1855, he visited the Muslim sacred cities of Mecca and Medina and became an accomplished linguist who knew some 36 languages.

Burton is best remembered for his translation from the Arabic of *The Arabian Nights* which he accomplished in 1850, but he also wrote more than a score of books on falconry and swordsmanship. In 1858 he was the first European to set eyes on Lake Tanganyika and the same year, together with John Speke, Burton made an unsuccessful attempt to find the source of the Nile.

Matthew Arnold

Matthew Arnold (1822 to 1888) was born in Laleham, Surrey, the eldest son of Dr Thomas Arnold of Rugby. Educated firstly at Winchester where he first started to write poetry, Matthew transferred to Rugby in 1837.

He read Classics on an open scholarship at Balliol in 1840. He started at Balliol in 1841, the same year that his father moved to Oxford to take up the post of Regius Professor of Modern History. Matthew won the Prize for English verse in 1843 with his poem *Cromwell* and obtained a Second Class degree in 1844.

After leaving Oxford, he returned to Rugby where he became a temporary assistant-master before being elected Fellow of Oriel from 1845 to 1850 and in 1851 he became a lay Inspector of Schools, an office from which he did not retire until 1886. Appropriately, the Matthew Arnold School is on the outskirts of Oxford, off Cumnor Hill.

Arnold made his name as a poet with *Poems: A New Edition* (1853-4), which included *The Scholar-Gipsy* and *Sohrab and Rustum*, and confirmed his standing as a poet with *New Poems* (1867), which contained *Dover Beach* and *Thyrsis*.

His major work on Oxford is *The Scholar-Gipsy* (1853) which is the story of a member of the University who fell in with a band of gypsies and travelled round with them, learning their lore and language. According to Joseph Glanvill of Exeter College, who was writing in the 17th century, there seems to have been a real scholar gypsy who was a student who went off with some travellers and successfully adopted their culture and way of life. In the poem Arnold mentions how 'near me on the grass lies Glanvill's book – '

Arnold introduces several references to the Oxford countryside, most of which are still recognisable. Maytime in Fifield, summer at the ferry at Bablockhithe and in the Wychwoods, harvest time at Godstow and, of course, Bagley Wood. The Gipsy looks down on the city from Cumnor (or 'Cumner' as Arnold spells it), one snowy night and has no difficulty in making out the lights in Christ Church Hall, some two and a half miles away. A tree known as the Poet's Tree still stands guard on a ridge overlooking Hinksey. Arnold referred to it as 'the signal-elm that looks on Ilsley Downs,' but in reality it is an oak.

A public house in Kennington, named the *Scholar Gipsy* in recognition of the hero's wanderings in and around Bagley Wood just outside the village, was demolished in 2001.

Another Oxford favourite, *Thyrsis* (1867), was written to commemorate the author's friend, Arthur Hugh Clough, who died at Florence in 1861 and includes the reference to the city's towers and spires which has become synonymous with Oxford.

And that sweet city with her dreaming spires,
She needs not June for beauty's heightening.
Lovely at all times she lies, lovely to-night!

Within walking distance are the two tiny villages of North and South Hinksey, Sandford and Wytham, and 'Cumner' once again. Further afield are 'Ensham' (the correct spelling at that time) and 'The signal-elm, that looks on Ilsley Downs,' in reality an oak tree.

Arnold was elected Professor of Poetry at Oxford in 1857, a post he held for ten years, and published several critical works, including *Essays in Criticism* (1865, 1888 which include the often-quoted lines referring to Oxford, 'Home of lost causes, and forsaken beliefs, and unpopular names, and impossible loyalties!') and *Culture and Anarchy* (1869) and books on religious themes such as *Literature and Dogma* (1872) and *Last Essays on Church and Religion* (1877).

When Arnold was in the process of delivering the Creweian Oration as Public Orator at the Encaenia of 1864, the advice of a student member of the audience was to 'Cut it short! Give him beer!' In 1870, at the ceremony for the installation of Lord Salisbury as Chancellor, Matthew Arnold was himself on the receiving end of a degree when he was awarded an honorary Doctorate of Civil Law. Thirteen years later he was voted a Civil List Pension of £250 a year 'in public recognition of service to the poetry and literature of England.'

Matthew Arnold died in Liverpool in April 1888 and was buried at Laleham where he was born. His portrait is in the Senior Common Room at Oriel.

Thomas Hughes

Although Thomas Hughes (1822 to 1896) was a member of Oriel College, his name does not appear in the list of University honours in the *Register to 1900*.

He is primarily remembered as the author of the very successful *Tom Brown's Schooldays, by An Old Boy,* and the less well-known *Tom Brown at Oxford*. Much of the early background for *Schooldays* (1857) reflects Hughes' own childhood as grandson of the vicar at Uffington and around the Vale of White Horse (not *the* White Horse!). Both the Vale and the administrative district of Oxfordshire are named after a figure cut into the Downs.

This white horse, which stands a few hundred metres north of the Ridgeway, is the oldest of the 15 such horses cut into the chalk downlands of England. No one is certain of its age or origins or if it is Iron Age or Saxon. The Iron Age theory derives from its obvious similarity to a horse found on coins from that time but others say that it marked a Saxon meeting place or tribal boundary. The theory that it was cut to commemorate Alfred the Great's victory over the Danes at the battle of Ashdown in 871 has yet to be proved, indeed the site of the battle itself remains unidentified.

The first written reference to the Horse appears in an 11th-century document from Abingdon Abbey and by the 14th century it was looked on as a major attraction, second only to Stonehenge.

Today, the Horse measures some 111 metres in length and 40 metres in height. It is little more than an elongated outline and the scourings which were carried out to prevent scrub invading it completely, together with erosion, have gradually altered its shape. Thomas Hughes gives a detailed account of the scouring of the White Horse which still takes place every 7 years and consists of hammering fresh chalk into the figure's outline. Nearby Uffington Castle is the venue for picnics, stalls selling old-fashioned food and drink, country games such as cheese rolling, plays, mumming, Morris dancing, and such jollification, as described in his *The Scouring of the White* Horse.

The Horse continues to be scoured to the accompaniment of very varied entertainments. On 24th and 25th June 2000, the Millennium celebrations (as advertised on the Internet) consisted of Mystery Plays, Tug-of-war, Bowling for a pig, Coconut Shy, Foot races for children, Races for cheeses, a Children's Pageant, Kite Flying, Mummers, Displays by the National Trust and a Display by the Flying Machines of the Red Arrows! Afterwards, a barn dance was held, for which the admission charge was 'set at £1 for each adult.' It is still considered lucky to stand on the Horse's eye and make a wish.

Hughes was called to the bar in 1848 and became a county court judge in 1882. He was a Liberal MP from 1865 to 1874 and became closely associated with the Christian Socialists, helping with the foundation of the Working Men's College (1854), of which he was Principal between 1872 and 1883. In 1880, he started a co-operative community in Rugby, Tennessee. It was envisaged as a class-free co-operative 'for younger sons of English gentry and others wishing to start life anew in America.' At its peak, there were about 350 inhabitants living in more than 70 buildings. This idyll failed to prosper on a long term basis and suffered a loss of £150,000, largely due to the fact that the land on which it was situated was fit for growing little but pine trees. According to its website, this 'would-Utopia survives today as both a living community and a fascinating historic site.'

In Uffington, Hughes lived in a house called the Hall which has been demolished, but the village hall is named after him and has a plaque to his memory. Tom Brown's School Museum, in Broad Street, illustrates the life and times of Hughes as well as exhibiting background material from the White Horse area.

Thomas Hughes' grandmother was a friend of Sir Walter Scott and it was she who supplied him with background information for his novel, *Kenilworth*, which includes the story of the life and death of Amy Robsart at Cumnor Hall and her burial in the University church of St Mary the Virgin. Prefixed to *Kenilworth* is the *Ballad of Cumnor Hall,* written by William Julius Mickle. Curiously, when the round barrow on White Horse Hill was excavated in 1856, one of the finds was an 1831 copy of Scott's *Demonology and Witchcraft,* buried there either as a joke or as a reference to the connection between *Kenilworth* and the Hughes family.

Scott himself visited Oxford and came away confused. In *The Adventures of Mr Verdant Green,* the author writes, 'But if such a shrewd and practised observer as Sir Walter Scott, after a week's hard and systematic sight-seeing, could only say of Oxford, 'The time has been much too short to convey to me separate and distinct ideas of all the variety of wonders that I saw: my memory only at present furnishes a grand but indistinct picture of towers, and chapels and oriels, and vaulted halls, and libraries, and paintings,' – if Sir Walter Scott could say this after a week's work, it is not to be wondered at that Mr Green senior, after so brief and rapid a survey of the city at the heels of an unintelligent guide, should feel himself slightly confused when, on his return to the Manor Green, he attempted to give a slight description of the wonderful sights of Oxford.'

It may be just a coincidence, or perhaps Sir Walter was attempting to clarify his recollections of Oxford, when the tenant of Frewin Hall, who was an old friend of the writer, insisted that he met him in the house some time after Scott's death.

Richard Doddridge Blackmore

Richard Doddridge Blackmore (1825 to 1900) was born at Longworth (then in Berkshire), as was Dean Fell of Christ Church whose baptism is recorded in the parish registers. Blackmore grew up at the Rectory at Elsfield before going up to Exeter College where he gained a Second in Classics in 1847. His novel *Lorna Doone,* published in 1869, was a great success and made his name as a writer; his other novels, such as *Cripps the Carrier* which is set on Otmoor, are largely unread.

Blackmore became a lawyer and was called to the bar, but did not practice as a barrister because he was epileptic and dreaded court appearances in case he suffered an attack. He therefor spent his career in working as a solicitor. He is buried in Exeter Cathedral.

Edward Bradley

Cuthbert Bede was the pen name of Edward Bradley (1827 to 1889). The author of *The Adventures of Mr. Verdant Green* was the son of a surgeon from Kidderminster, Worcestershire. Edward attended Kidderminster Grammar School, and then went to University College, Durham, on a Foundation Scholarship, in 1845.

The following year Bradley adopted the pseudonym 'Cuthbert Bede', an amalgamation of Durham's two patrons, St. Cuthbert and the Venerable Bede. He used it for the rest of his life and it became an alter ego. Bradley took his BA in 1848 and stayed on at Durham to prepare for a Licentiateship in Theology. Significantly, when he signed his drawings with a 'BA' after his name, Bradley chose to omit the word 'Dunelm', allowing it to be assumed that the BA might equally have been 'Oxon.' or 'Cantab'.

Although it would have been possible for him to use a guide book and directory to describe Oxford life, it would be very unlikely that he would have been able to name drop as casually and accurately as Bradley does. No-one could have drawn so efficiently the exteriors and interiors of Oxford without a considerable residence during term, as Bradley would have needed access to everyday scenes within the privacy of colleges and other University buildings in order to be so realistic.

How *The Adventures of Mr. Verdant Green* came to be written is complicated and controversial. Bradley explains 'I proposed to adapt the sketches to Oxford of which I knew a little – and be[tween] the life in which and the life at [University] Coll. Durham (at *that* time) [I do not] know what it is now I really saw very little difference.' At last, the publisher Nathaniel Cooke accepted the work. All three 1850s editions were shilling paperbacks called 'books for the rail' because they were sold on station bookstalls. When they appeared in a sixpenny edition, sales more than doubled. It is said that the great Oxonian, Edward Pusey, kept a copy in his rooms at Christ Church.

In 1849, Bradley left Durham and at the earliest opportunity, November, 1850, he was ordained to the curacy of Whittlesea Mere, Huntingdonshire. The same year, his book of sketches, *College Life*, appeared, followed by letters and sketches for *Punch*, and the first part of the *Adventures,* in 1853. The *Further Adventures* came out in 1854, and the following year Bradley moved to another curacy near Malvern, the former parish of the supposed original of the character Verdant Green.

He soon moved to Bobbington in Staffordshire, where he produced the final part of the trilogy, *Married and Done For*, and all three books appeared in one volume in 1857. By then a married man himself, the Bradleys moved to a final curacy in 1859 at Denton with Caldecote, Huntingdonshire. In 1870, it was suggested that he should write another Verdant Green-type series, set in Cambridge instead of Oxford. He replied, 'My 'Verdant Green' has already been an obstacle to me in my clerical profession – chiefly, however, with those who are personally ignorant of me – and who only know me as the author of 'Verdant Green'. Until I am safe in a living which shall be mine for life, I should not care to issue another tale of a similar nature to 'Verdant Green.' This laying the blame of Bradley's failure to gain his own living at the feet of Mr. Verdant Green does not appear to have been justified. He declines to blame his other less than literary efforts such as the *Ratcatcher's Daughter.*

In 1871 Bradley finally obtained the living of Stretton, in Rutland, where he felt in a position to produce *Little Mr. Bouncer and his Friend Verdant Green.* It is not, however, a sequel to the trilogy although it features the same characters, with a rearrangement of situations, and a change of hero. If Bradley had hoped to capitalise – perhaps socially as much as financially – on the success of his earlier best seller he was disappointed for this was not to be the case.

The *Verdant Green* trilogy may be taken as an accurate representation of Oxford in the middle of the nineteenth century. Bradley was not afraid of his work being criticised by 'real' Oxonians, and there are no contemporary accusations of inaccuracy.

Bradley's last years are relatively obscure and by 1889, after a prolonged period of general ill health, Edward Bradley had pleurisy in both lungs. He lived until 12th December 1889, and was buried in his old parish of Stretton, Rutland.

Charles Lutwidge Dodgson

Charles Lutwidge Dodgson (1832 to 1898) was born in the Rectory Daresbury, Cheshire, the son of a clergyman. At an early age he would write stories and other forms of entertainment for his brother and seven sisters. He came up to Christ Church in 1851 to read Mathematics and obtained a Third Class in Classics and a First in Mathematics three years later. He was to spend the rest of his life at Christ Church, being appointed Mathematics Examiner in 1863 and Moderator five years later.

He was a self-effacing man and would stammer under pressure, a fact of which he was only too aware. He used to refer to himself as the Dodo from his saying 'Do-do-Dodgson' when under stress. This condition might explain his ability to make friends with children more easily than with adults. Included in his 'white stone' (red-letter) days, were photographic sessions and boating trips in the company of youngsters, his favourites being the three Liddell sisters, the daughters of the Dean of Christ Church. Dodgson enjoyed playing with words and the characters in his stories indulge in nonsensical conversations full of puns and topical references to Oxford luminaries of the day. In *Confessions of a Caricaturist*, the illustrator Harry Furniss wrote 'Carroll was not selfish, but a liberal-minded, liberal-handed egotist, but his egotism was all but second childhood.'

Dodgson was the talented and knowledgeable photographer of such leading Oxonians as Ruskin, Tennyson and Rossetti and had his own studio in college on the roof of his rooms in Tom Quad, Christ Church's large front quadrangle. Some of his photographic apparatus is now in the Museum of the History of Science in the Old Ashmolean Building, in Broad Street.

When they read the manuscript of *Alice's Adventures Underground,* Dodgson's friends urged him to publish it in book form. It appeared with the title *Alice's Adventures in Wonderland* and the pen name Lewis Carroll, in 1865. The advice was good, so good that *Alice* has appeared in most of the world's major languages plus Latin, Esperanto, Braille and shorthand.

Its sequel, *Alice Through the Looking-Glass*, of 1871, was written specifically for publication, with a much more sophisticated readership in mind. Both books were originally illustrated by Tenniel. All of Dodgson's stories may be read on more than one level: as amusement, nonsense, allegory, or satire.

He continued to publish learned mathematical treatises under his own name and seems to have been a little sensitive about his 'double-life.' It is said that he was in the habit of returning unopened any letters which were addressed to Lewis Carroll. An amusing story is told of how Queen Victoria, a great admirer of the *Alice* books, once requested that she be sent a copy of Dodgson's next book as soon as it was published. The writer readily agreed. One can imagine the Queen's surprise and disappointment when she eagerly unwrapped the parcel only to find a book on mathematics!

Dodgson died on 14th January 1898, shortly before his 66th birthday, while visiting his sister in Guildford. In 1948 the original manuscript of *Alice* was given to the British Museum by the Librarian of Congress, Dr Luther H Evans, as 'a gift from America to the British people at the end of a hard and bitter war.' It had fetched $50,000 at auction.

Many places in and around Oxford have Carroll connections, notably Alice's Shop at 83 St Aldate's, where Alice would pop across from Christ Church to buy barley sugar. It was formerly known as 'Alice's Sheep Shop' from the elderly sheep who was in charge of it in *Through the Looking-Glass*, sitting there busily doing her knitting with glasses perched on the end of her nose. The old shop sign included a picture of this sheep shopkeeper.

On the other side of the road, by the side of Folly Bridge, is the boatyard from which Dodgson and the girls set off for their trip to Godstow Lock on 4th July 1862, the day when the writer began to invent Wonderland. They picnicked at Godstow and afterwards Alice pleaded with Dodgson to write down all that he had told them about *Alice's Adventure Underground,* as they were initially called.

In the churchyard of the hamlet of Binsey, not far from Godstow, is St Margaret's well which features in the stories as the home of the three girls written in to represent the Liddell sisters. The steps down to the water were built by the Reverend Thomas Prout in 1874 and a tablet records the gift. The well water, still said by some to be beneficial to those with eye complaints, is the origin of the Binsey Treacle Well. This concept so caught the imagination of Lewis Carroll that he introduced it into the conversation at the Mad Tea Party. The derivation of the word treacle is really *theriaca*, Latin for antidote, due to its healing powers. The well is shown in a Pre-Raphaelite stained glass window in the Cathedral which shows the life of Oxford's patron saint, Fridewide. She is said to have caused the spring to erupt in order to bathe the eyes of an over zealous suitor whom she had caused to go blind in order to stop him pestering her.

The Liddell sisters were taken around the City and University for education and pleasure and their visits would include the Botanic Garden, Magdalen Grove to see the deer and the newly built University Museum of Natural History where there is a dodo reconstructed from some remains of the bird, together with its portrait.

Dodgson's own portrait hangs in Christ Church Hall along with the usual collection of the great and the good, including the college's Founder, Henry VIII. More unusual is the Alice window which gives Dodgson's dates and places of birth and death, along with portraits of the White Rabbit, the March Hare, the Dormouse, The Red Queen, the Duchess, the Griffin, the Mock Turtle, the Caterpillar, the Cheshire Cat and, of course, the Dodo.

William Morris

William Morris (1834 to 1896) was born in Walthamstow, the third of the nine children of a well-to-do family. He entered Exeter College where he met Edward Burne-Jones, who was to become his life-long friend. Neither took a degree. In spite of this, Morris was offered the Professorship of Poetry which he refused. He was made an honorary Fellow of Exeter College in 1883.

At Oxford, Morris's loving of things medieval was intensified by coming into contact with others with the same interests, all of them heavily influenced by the works of writers such as Tennyson, Carlyle and Ruskin. Together, they created an idealised world full of supposedly medieval ideals, which in time, they were to extend to include art, architecture and their own writing. This was the basis of the ideals of the Pre-Raphaelite Brotherhood.

Left: Alice window in Christ Church (CL Dodgson)

In 1855, when he was 21 and came into some money, Morris joined Burne-Jones for a walking tour of the great gothic cathedrals of northern France. They both abandoned their intentions of becoming clergymen to become artists instead, and Morris left Oxford at the end of that year. In 1857, Morris, Burne-Jones and Dante Gabriel Rossetti, together with a group of their friends, painted the frescoes in the Old Library of the Oxford Union Society complex in St Michael's Street. These have been recently renovated after near destruction by the effects of time. Chaucer and the Icelandic sagas, of which he made translations, influenced Morris's work. He also produced illuminated manuscripts which could compare with fine medieval specimens.

About this time Morris met Jane Burden, the daughter of an ostler from Holywell, who modelled for Dante Gabriel Rossetti. He married her in St Michael at the North Gate church on 26th April 1859, where a copy of the entry in the parish registers is on display in the church's Treasury. Jane was only 20 and lived with her parents in Brooks Yard. Once she was married and moved in more polite society, she hid her humble origins to the extent of not even returning to Oxford for her own mother's funeral.

In the 1870s, Morris and Rossetti were joint tenants of Kelmscott Manor where Rossetti managed to secure the favours of Mrs Morris and they lived at Kelmscott Manor from 1871 until Morris's death in 1896. This Grade 1 listed Tudor building by the Thames was constructed in 1570 and stands on the edge of the village. To Morris it appeared to have 'grown out of the soil' with its 'quaint garrets amongst great timbers of the roof where of old times the tillers and herdsmen slept,' and this delighted him. Set into the wall of a house in the village is a stone depicting Morris with his portly figure, characteristic beard and shock of hair, sitting alongside his dovecote. On seeing it the visitor will not find it difficult to understand why Ruskin was able to write of Morris in 1879 'I can't understand how a

Right: St Michael's church Treasury (William Morris)

man who . . . enjoys dinner – and breakfast – and supper – to that extent of fat – can write such lovely poems about Misery.'

The Morris family, William, Janey, who died in 1914, and their daughters Jane and May are buried in Kelmscott churchyard.

A good description of the house and village as it was in Morris's day, which he wrote himself, can be found in *The Quest* Number IV. November 1895 and is entitled 'Gossip about an old house on the Upper Thames.' In his book, *News from Nowhere*, which appeared in 1892, there is a woodcut showing the manor as well as a description of it.

Morris's daughter May lived at the manor until 1938. The house was restored in 1963–6 and the Pre-Raphaelite wallpaper is still intact. Kelmscott Manor is open by appointment only.

In 1876, Morris was visiting the great medieval church at Burford which was then being restored by the architect GE Street who considered this one of his greatest achievements. Morris was horrified to discover what was being done to the church. He particularly objected to Street's love of high pitched roofs; at Burford he replaced the flat oak of the chancel roof with the typically High Victorian variety. Street also destroyed the medieval wall painting of St Christopher, which had escaped the attentions of Puritan fanatics, because it did not fit in with his own narrow views on what was beautiful. When Morris challenged the Vicar to account for this vandalism, this worthy replied, 'the church, sir, is mine and, if I choose to, I shall stand on my head in it.' Morris was on his way to Broadway, but stopped off to write an indignant letter which paved the way for the formation in 1877 of the Society for the Protection of Ancient Buildings. This work was to become one of the passions of Morris's life. In 1977, its centenary year, the Society visited Burford church to mark the occasion.

Algernon Swinburne

Algernon Swinburne (1837 to 1909) was a member of Balliol and became associated with the Pre-Raphaelite Brotherhood. Leaving Oxford without a degree, he travelled in Europe, and throughout his life spent a great deal of time in Northumberland, which he called the 'crowning county' of England. He achieved success with his play *Atalanta in Calydon* (1865), and the first of his series of *Poems and Ballads* (1865) took the public by storm. Other works include *Songs before Sunrise* (1871) and *Essays and Studies* (1875). In 1879, after a breakdown caused by alcoholism, a friend took care of him, Theodore Watts-Dunton, and he lived as something of a recluse for the rest of his life. He published more than 20 books of poetry, drama and prose, which included critical works on Shakespeare, Victor Hugo and Ben Jonson. Swinburne's opinion of Oxford life expressed the idea that people in Oxford could not be said to die 'for they never begin to live.'

Walter Pater

Walter Pater (1839 to 1894) took a Second in Classics from the Queen's College in 1862 before being elected a Fellow of Brasenose in 1864. He held this position until his death thirty years afterwards but did not work as a tutor at Brasenose for the last ten years of his life as he then lived in London.

Despite his quiet and retiring life-style, Pater's work became known as an example of 'art for art's sake' and his influence widespread. The subject matter was largely the art and literature of the Renaissance and he was known as an aesthete and, because of this, he influenced members of the aesthetic movement including Oscar Wilde.

Among Pater's best-known work is *Marius the Epicurian* of which the hero is a young Roman who lived in the second century AD.

Thomas Hardy

The novelist and poet Thomas Hardy (1840 to 1928) was born in Upper Bockhampton, Dorset. After going to school in Dorchester, he became an architect and at 22 moved to London. There, he started to write poems which show his love of country life. Unsuccessful with his poetry, Hardy began to write novels, beginning with *Far from the Madding Crowd* which was published in 1874. He then became a professional writer and a series of novels followed: *The Return of the Native* (1878), *The Mayor of Casterbridge* (1886), *Tess of the D'Urbervilles* (1891) and *Jude the Obscure* in 1896. Hardy then resumed his poetry, as well as the epic drama, *The Dynasts* (1903–8). Several novels have been filmed, *Far from the Madding Crowd* (Schlesinger, 1967) and *Tess* (Polanski, 1979).

Thomas Hardy's last novel, *Jude the Obscure,* had the distinction of being burned by the Bishop of Wakefield, who succeeded in getting it banned from Smith's Circulating Library as immoral.

Wantage features in *Jude* as Alfredston, Christminster is Oxford and Cresscombe Letcombe Bassett. The last is the village where Arabella seduces Jude after he meets her washing pigs' offal in Letcombe Brook and their shotgun wedding is brought about. The so-called 'Arabella's Walk' takes in Segsbury Camp, Letcombe Regis and Letcombe Bassett itself and includes part of the Ridgeway where the couple would walk before their marriage.

In *Jude* Hardy shows both sides of late-Victorian Christminster, beginning with the idealism of the young Jude who is living with his aunt in the Berkshire Downs. His romanticised views on the place are endorsed by the description given by a local labourer (who has himself never been there) as being full of learning, music and religion, for 'they raise pa'sons there like radishes in a bed.' To Jude, at this stage in his life, the voice of the city is the sound of bells which is carried on the breeze.

Hardy knew all too well, though, the other Oxford, with its sour-smelling, poverty-stricken courts and alleyways, all very un-Arnold and easy prey to cholera and other epidemic diseases. He also understood the uneasy relationship between Town and Gown, for, although Jude desperately wants to be accepted by a college, he is not above being a graffitist and chalks his comments on the wall of the college which has offered him sound but unwelcome advice. JIM Stewart relates how the Provost of Oriel of his day, Dr Phelps, told him that the College's Governing Body once considered suing Hardy for libel because an illustration on the title-page of *Jude* looked very like Oriel's Front Quad, and so might imply that it had been a former Provost who had given this advice. Stewart did not entirely believe this snippet of information and neither, he suspected, did the Provost himself.

Hardy worked in Oxford as assistant architect at St Barnabas' church in the exclusively working-class suburb of Jericho. 'Barnie' church comes into the novel as 'St Silas' and Jericho as 'Beersheba.' Many other Oxford names are there in disguise: Biblioll for Balliol, Cardinal for Christ Church, Remembrance Day for Commemoration, Fourways for Carfax and so on. Jude surveys the Promised Land from the 'octagonal chamber in the lantern of a singularly-built theatre' and so may we if we climb up to the cupola of the Sheldonian. Jude is saddened by the condition of the buildings, some of the colleges being like 'vaults above ground,' while Mildew Lane and Sarcophagus College speak for themselves. Nevertheless, the hero is spellbound by all the Gothic which surrounds him.

The writer shows the amount of interest then shown by Town when anything remotely noteworthy is being done by Gown. During Commemoration Week, for example, country people bring picnics to eat in college gardens and quadrangles as if visiting a stately home, which, in a way, they are. Jude's stonemason mates go off to the river on a fine summer's afternoon as he lies dying.

Altogether, the novel conveys the strange mixture of privilege and poverty, with the young gentlemen and their dainty womenfolk taking

tea in college while the labourers chat to the light ladies in the pubs of Beersheba. Contemporary Victoriana combines uneasily with medieval relics to produce a claustrophobic, unwholesome atmosphere.

Hardy was given an honorary Doctorate of Literature in 1921 and made an honorary Fellow of the Queen's College. In this sense, Jude may be said to have obtained his degree at last.

The pub in Walton Street now known as Jude the Obscure was opened at about the same time that the novel appeared, but until recently it was named the Prince of Wales. Towards the end of the 20th century, it was decided to change its name and the suggestion of Jude accepted. This was decided on partly because of the novel's associations with the Jericho area, partly in recognition that many students of Jude's social origins are now at the University.

Andrew Lang

Andrew Lang (1844 to 1912) was born in Selkirk and attended Edinburgh Academy and the Universities of St Andrew's and Glasgow before coming up to Balliol, where he took a First in Classics in 1868, and went on to be a Fellow of Merton from 1868 to 1874.

His earliest published work was *The Ballads and Lyrics of Old France* (1872), which was followed by other similar volumes. Other writings include historical and anthropological studies like *Myth, Ritual and Religion* (1887) and *The Making of Religion* (1898), which brought him into conflict with the anthropologist James G Frazer. Lang also wrote novels and a series of children's books, the first being *The Blue Fairy Book* (1889).

Andrew Lang was a very competent classicist as he proved in

Left: 'Barnie' church (Thomas Hardy)

Homer and the Epic (1893) and *Homer and his Age* (1906), and in his translations of Theocritus, Bion, and Moschus (1880), *Homeric Hymns* (1899), and his contributions to versions of the *Odyssey* (1879) and the *Iliad* (1883). Lang also wrote *Oxford, brief historical and descriptive notes,* 1882, a book on Oxford as it was in his day. He received an honorary D Litt at the installation of Viscount Goschen as Chancellor in 1904.

Gerard Manley Hopkins

Gerard Manley Hopkins (1844 to 1889) was born in Stratford, Essex and went to Balliol where he got a First in Classics in 1867. Influenced by the Oxford Movement in general and John Henry Newman in particular, he became a Catholic in 1866 while still an undergraduate. He studied for the priesthood with the Jesuits in North Wales and was ordained in 1877. He worked as a parish priest in London, in Oxford, in a slum area of Liverpool, and in Glasgow and later taught at Stonyhurst. Hopkins became Professor of Greek Literature at University College, Dublin in 1884, but resigned the post after some five years.

None of Hopkins' poems was published in his lifetime; it is said that this was deliberately engineered by his superiors in the Church. His friend and literary executor, Robert Bridges, published an edition in 1918, which was given a very mixed reception, notably to Hopkins' experiments with 'sprung rhythm'; however, a new and expanded edition in 1930 was widely acclaimed, and his work became influential. His best-known poems include *The Wreck of the Deutschland* and *The Windhover.*

Apart from his Balliol connections, Hopkins was assistant priest at the church of St Aloysius in the Woodstock Road, Oxford, where he is commemorated by a holy water stoup.

St Aloysius' exterior (GM Hopkins)

He has left some literary memoirs of the city of which probably the best known is *Duns Scotus's Oxford*:

> Towery city and branchy between towers;
> Cuckoo-echoing, bell-swarmed, lark-charmed, rook-racked,
> river-rounded;
> The dapple-eared lily below thee; that country and town did
> Once encounter in, here coped and poised powers.

And on *Binsey Poplars, felled 1879*:

> After-comers cannot guess the beauty been,
> Ten or twelve, only ten or twelve
> Strokes of havoc unselve
> The sweet especial scene,
> Rural scene, a rural scene,
> Sweet especial rural scene.

It is good to relate that Hopkins' trees were replaced by the Oxford Civic Society who planted British black poplars at Binsey.

And also:

> Thou hast a base and brickish skirt there, sours
> That neighbour-nature thy grey beauty is grounded
> Best in; graceless growth, thou hast confounded
> Rural rural keeping – folk, flocks, and flowers.

The reference to the 'base and brickish skirt' is a condemnation of Jude's Jericho, built to accommodate workers at the University Press, artisans, minor tradesmen, college servants and railwaymen's families in rows of redbrick terraced houses.

Chapter Six

Robert Bridges ✍ Mrs Humphrey Ward ✍ Oscar Wilde;

Brandon Thomas ✍ John Meade Falkner ✍ Kenneth Grahame;

A E Housman ✍ Jerome K Jerome

Robert Bridges

Robert Bridges (1844 to 1930) was born at Walmer in Kent and went to Corpus Christi where he took a Second in Classics in 1867, before he went on to study medicine at St Bartholomew's Hospital in London. He practised as a doctor until 1881 when he gave up medicine for writing. He worked among the underprivileged, and their courageous attitude to life had an influence on Bridges' writing.

Although he produced works on Milton (1893) and Keats (1895), it is Bridges' own poetry for which he is best known; he was Poet Laureate from 1913 to 1930. From 1907 onwards he lived at Boar's Hill and was the first of the literary fraternity to colonise the place.

Mrs Humphrey Ward

Mary Augusta Arnold or Mrs Humphrey Ward (1851 to 1920) was born in Hobart, Tasmania. A granddaughter of the great Dr Arnold of Rugby and niece of Matthew Arnold, she came to England with her family in 1856. In 1872, she married a Fellow of Brasenose, Thomas

Humphrey Ward by whose name she is usually referred.

Mary lived for some nine years in Oxford during which time she met George Elliot and walked in Merton College garden with her one day in the early summer of 1870 while the novelist was on a visit to the Rector of Lincoln College, Mark Pattison.

The Humphrey Wards moved to London where Mary had her first book published in 1871. This was *Millie and Ollie*; her second, *Robert Elsmere* (1888), was an immediate success. In her day, Mary Humphrey Ward was one of the country's leading novelists with *The History of David Grieve* in 1892, *Marcella*, 1894, *Sir George Tressaday* in 1896, *Helbeck of Bannisdale*, 1898, *Eleanor*, 1900 and in 1903 *Lady Rose's Daughter*. The theme of her books was social reform and the need to help the underprivileged.

Strange as it may seem today, she opposed women being given the vote, became the first President of the Anti-Suffrage League and played an active part in preventing the extension of the suffrage to women. Instead of encouraging young women to involve themselves in the world around them, she wrote numerous articles against votes for women and included this subject in her novels, notably *The Testing of Diana Mallory* (1908) and *Delia Blanchflower* in 1915. Her son, Arnold Ward, the Conservative MP for Watford, extended her campaign. It was he who marred his mother's last years with debts incurred by his addiction to gambling.

Mary's sister Julia died in 1908, leaving behind two young sons, Julian and Aldous Huxley on whom she lavished care and affection.

Mrs Humphrey Ward's autobiography, *A Writer's Recollections*, appeared in 1918.

Oscar Wilde

Oscar Fingal O'Flahertie Wills Wilde (1854 to 1900) was born in Dublin. His father, Sir William Wilde, was an eye and ear surgeon and his mother, Jane, wrote poetry under the pen name Speranza. Oscar Wilde gained a scholarship to Trinity College, Dublin, where he became an excellent classicist. In 1874, he won a scholarship to Magdalen College, where he came under the influence of aesthete John Ruskin. In 1875, while on holiday in Italy, Wilde began to write poetry, and in 1878, he won the University's Newdigate Prize for English verse for his epic poem, *Ravenna*. He also took a First in Classics the same year.

During his years at Magdalen, Wilde cultivated his reputation for increasingly flamboyant behaviour, dress and speech. 'I never approve, or disapprove, of anything now,' he once said. 'It is an absurd attitude to take towards life. We are not sent into the world to air our moral prejudices. I never take any notice of what common people say and I never interfere with what charming people do.'

Oscar Wilde married Constance Lloyd in May 1884. During the early years of their marriage, they had two sons, Cyril and Vyvyan. Wilde became a leading literary figure of the Aesthetic Movement at the turn of the century; unfortunately he was also involved in a highly controversial law suit due to his homosexual activities with the heir of the Marquis of Queensbury. This resulted in his being convicted of 'gross indecency' and condemned to two years hard labour about which he wrote in *The Ballad of Reading Gaol*. After he was released from gaol, Wilde's marriage to Constance was virtually over, although it was never legally terminated.

Wilde died bankrupt on November 30, 1900 and was buried in the Bagneux Cemetery. His body was reinterred in the Pere-Lachaise Cemetery in Paris in 1909.

Brandon Thomas

Brandon Thomas (1857 to 1914) is best known for his masterpiece, *Charley's Aunt*, which is always staged in the clothes of the original period, 1892. The first London run was for 4 years. The expected upper class characters are represented by a Colonel, a Lord and Donna Lucia (that is, the Aunt herself) The play is set in and around the fictional St Olde's College and the first scene in the hero's rooms carries a very specific description of its furnishings and belongings, such as pictures of Eights, champagne bottles, cigar boxes and photographs of chorus girls.

John Meade Falkner

John Meade Falkner (1858 to 1932) was born in Manningford Bruce in Wiltshire. His father, the village curate, was a classical scholar whose lack of ambition to rise in the Church disguised his academic ability. John was taught Latin by his mother when he was only 5 years old, followed the next year by Greek lessons from his father. He went to school at Hardye's School in Dorchester, Dorset, then to Weymouth Grammar School. From 1873 to 1877, Falkner went to Marlborough College where he started to write poetry.

In 1878 he went up to Hertford College to read Modern History and finished with a Third. Besides getting a degree, however, he learned much about life and acquired several more languages. He also explored the Oxfordshire countryside and, in particular, fell in love with Burford.

After he left Oxford, Falkner moved to County Durham as tutor to John Noble, the son of Andrew Noble, chairman of the Armstrong

Right: Burford skyline (J Meade Falkner)

Whitworth Company. He became a friend of the Noble family, worked for the company, and eventually became its chairman.

Falkner's first book, *A Pocket Guide to Oxfordshire*, came out in 1894 and some of his poetry is included in *The Oxford Book of Contemporary Verse*. *The Lost Stradivarius* appeared in 1895 and his best loved work, the classic children's novel, *Moonfleet*, the following year. *Moonfleet* was adapted for television in 1986. In 1899, Falkner produced *A History of Oxfordshire*, which was followed by *A Pocket Guide to Berkshire* in 1902.

After he retired from Armstrong Whitworth, Falkner became involved in Durham University where he was Honorary Reader in Palaeography and the Cathedral where he held the position of Honorary Librarian to the Dean and Chapter. In 1927, he was given an honorary Fellowship of his old college, Hertford, something which meant a great deal to him.

John Noble and Falkner remained friends for the rest of their lives and became involved in the preservation of Burford's heritage. They donated the statues of the Virgin Mary and the Archangel Gabriel which stand on either side of the high altar in the church of St John the Baptist, the reredos in the Lady Chapel, the stone screen which surrounds it and the flooring. In addition, there are two Italian altar frontals on the wall of the north aisle and other decorations. Also in the Lady Chapel are two windows that commemorate Falkner and Andrew Noble. In the south transept is glass of 1907 with a Latin inscription which reads, 'Pray for the good estate of three Johns who have loved this church – John Leggare, John Noble and John Meade Falkner.'

Falkner died in 1932 and his ashes were interred in the tomb of his brother who had been buried in the churchyard at Burford in 1903. This 'bale' tomb is the one to the furthest east of those in the churchyard.

Kenneth Grahame

Kenneth Grahame (1859 to 1932) was born in Edinburgh, but was sent to Berkshire to live with relatives after the death of his mother in 1864. From the age of 9 until he was 16, Grahame went to St Edward's School in Oxford's Woodstock Road, where there is a window to his memory. He entered the Bank of England in 1879, became its secretary in 1898, but retired for health reasons in 1908.

The characters Ratty, Badger, Mole and Toad originated in a series of bedtime stories and letters to his son Alistair and like *Alice in Wonderland,* were not written with publication in mind. *The Wind in the Willows* was published as a complete story in 1908. Set on and around the Thames around Mapledurham where Grahame is thought to have been inspired by the rosy brick Mapledurham House to create Toad Hall. The illustrations by Shepherd certainly do show a resemblance.

Alistair grew up to become an undergraduate at Christ Church. Grahame himself lived in Blewbury, in the Vale of White Horse from 1910 to 1924, in a Tudor farmhouse called Bohan's. He also lived for a time in Church Cottage in Pangbourne, across the Thames in Berkshire), in the heart of Toad, Rat and Mole country where EH Shepard, the original illustrator of *Wind in the Willows,* would come for inspiration.

The Wind in the Willows was dramatised in 1930 by AA Milne as *Toad of Toad Hall.* Toad sings immodestly:

> The clever men at Oxford,
> Know all there is to be knowed,
> But none of them knows one half as much,
> As intelligent Mr Toad.

The gentleness of *The Wind in the Willows* belies the conditions of writer's personal life. Grahame's marriage was an unhappy one and

Discovering Literary Oxfordshire

Alistair died in 1920 when he threw himself under a train near Port Meadow. Father and son are buried in one grave in Oxford's Holywell cemetery. Their grave is to the right of the pathway on entering the cemetery; Kenneth's epitaph is on the near side of the gravestone, Alistair's on the reverse. It has an epitaph by Anthony Hope Hawkins which speaks of 'the beautiful memory' of Grahame and says that Alistair, who was buried on his birthday, has now crossed the river.

A E Housman

A(lfred) E(dward) Housman (1859 to 1936) was born in Fockbury, Worcestershire, the eldest of seven children. He came up St. John's College in 1877, where, after a promising start and in spite of getting a First in Classics Mods in 1879, he failed to gain a final honours degree. His failure was considered sufficient cause for Housman leave academia and go off to London to become a civil servant.

The death of his mother when he was 12 years old upset Housman so much that, according to his sister, death started to obsess him.

A Shropshire Lad appeared in 1896 and after moving to London Housman began his classical studies once more. So successful was he that the reviews and articles on Greek and Roman authors which he produced were of such undeniable scholarship that he was elected to the Professorship of Latin at London University in 1892, a position which he held until 1911. In that year Housman moved to Cambridge to become Professor of Latin, where, as a Fellow of Trinity College, he continued to publish editions of Latin authors and essays of textual criticism.

In 1922, Housman published a new volume of 41 *Last Poems*, most of which were written between 1895 and 1910; *More Poems were* published by Houseman's brother in 1936, after the poet's death.

Jerome K Jerome

Jerome Klapka Jerome (1859 to 1927) was born in Walsall, Staffordshire and brought up in the East End of London. He was successively a clerk, schoolmaster, reporter, actor, and journalist, then became joint editor of *The Idler* (1892) and started his own weekly, *To-Day*. However, he is best remembered as the author of *Three Men in a Boat* (1887), a book which charts the adventures of the writer, George, Harris and Montmorency the dog as they row their way up the Thames from Kingston on Thames to Oxford, stopping off at towns and villages on the way.

The Barley Mow at Clifton Hampden features in the novel and is described when the three men tie up at its landing stage. Although badly damaged by fire in 1975, this thatched pub has been lovingly restored to approximately how one imagines it from the description given by Jerome.

Barley Mow, Clifton Hampden (Jerome K Jerome)

Here is Jerome on some Oxfordshire places:

On Dorchester, 'It is very old, and it was very strong and great once. Now it sits aside from the stirring world, and nods and dreams.'

and :

'Round Clifton Hampden, itself a wonderfully pretty village, old-fashioned, peaceful, and dainty with flowers, the river scenery is rich and beautiful,'

and:

'Abingdon is a typical country town of the smaller order – quiet, eminently respectable, clean, and desperately dull. It prides itself on being old, but whether it can compare in this respect with Wallingford and Dorchester seems doubtful. A famous abbey stood here once, and within what is left of its sanctified walls they brew a bitter ale nowadays.'

and:

'We spent two very pleasant days at Oxford. There are plenty of dogs in the town of Oxford. Montmorency had eleven fights on the first day, and fourteen on the second, and evidently thought he had got to Heaven.'

The Jerome family lived at Gould's Grove (or Troy) an old farmhouse about 1.5 miles southeast of Ewelme. He is buried, together with his wife and daughter, under a stone which reads *For we are labourers together with God.*

Chapter Seven

William Butler Yeats ✍ John Galsworthy ✍ Laurence Binyon

Hilaire Belloc ✍ John Fothergill ✍ Flora Thompson

Edward Thomas ✍ John Masefield ✍ Max Beerbohm

Lady Otteline Morrell ✍ Sir Winston Churchill ✍ John Buchan

Joyce Cary ✍ Compton Mackenzie

William Butler Yeats

William Butler Yeats (1865 to 1939) lived with his wife at 5 Broad Street, Oxford, from 1919 to 1921, in a house which occupied the site of the present Boswell's store. Despite a storm of protest, this house was torn down when Boswell's department store was built in 1928. Yeats moved in Oxfordshire circles which included William Morris and other Pre-Raphaelites, Lady Otteline Morrell and Oscar Wilde.

The Yeats later moved to Shillingford, where they rented Minchen's Cottage on the Warborough Road, and then to Thame, where a plaque on the wall of Cuttlebrook House at 42 High Street records their occupancy.

In 1921, the year of the creation of the Irish Free State, Yeats was invited to the Oxford Union Society to speak about self-government for Ireland. This he is said to have done by marching up and down, shaking his fists. He remarked that *Sinn Fein* had brought justice to his part of Ireland for the first time in centuries. In 1923 Yeats was elected senator in the first government of the Free State and also received the

Nobel Prize for Literature; in 1931 Oxford University conferred on him an honorary D Litt.

John Galsworthy

John Galsworthy (1867 to 1933) was born in Kingston Hill, Surrey. He went to New College where he got a Second in Jurisprudence in 1889. He was called to the bar in 1890, but chose to travel and become a writer. Galsworthy's novels were social accounts of their age. The six novels which make up *The Forsyte Saga* (1906–28), are about the wealthy middle-classes of the years before the First World War. The *Saga* became essential television viewing in the Sixties and another version was shown in 2002–3.

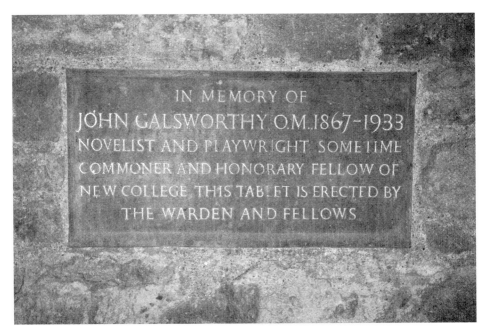

Galsworthy plaque, New College

Galsworthy was awarded the Nobel Prize for Literature in 1932 and an honorary D Litt from Oxford University in 1931. There is a plaque to his memory in the Cloisters of New College and also a college Scholarship was introduced in his name. When unveiling the plaque to the writer, John Masefield commented that he had never met such gentleness and pity for the poor and the unhappy in any man as in John Galsworthy.

Laurence Binyon

(Robert) Laurence Binyon (1869 to 1943) was born in Lancaster and came up to Trinity College where he won the Newdigate Prize for English verse in 1890 with his poem *Persephone* and took a Second in Classics two years later.

Binyon obtained a post in the British Museum, specialising in the art of China and Japan, and then left to go off to the Great War. After the war ended, he returned to work in the Museum. He published studies of Botticelli, Blake and other artists but his best known work is the poem *For the Fallen* which he wrote in 1914. Although they may not be aware of the name of either the author or the poem, virtually every adult in the country will recognise the lines from Remembrance Day Services:

> They shall not grow old, as we that are left grow old:
> Age shall not weary them, nor the years condemn.
> At the going down of the sun and in the morning
> We will remember them.

Laurence Binyon was awarded an honorary Doctorate of Literature from Oxford in 1933.

Hilaire Belloc

(Joseph) Hilaire (Pierre) Belloc (1870 to 1953) was born in St Cloud near Paris, the son of a French barrister and his English wife. The family moved to England during the Franco-Prussian war, and Hilaire went to the Oratory School, Birmingham, under Newman. He went on to Oxford in 1892 where he took a First in History from Balliol three years later. Two years of Belloc's Balliol career had been spent under the Mastership of Benjamin Jowett, who was able to inspire sufficient *esprit de corps* into the college for the sometimes satirical Belloc to write in a most unOxonian way in *To the Balliol Men Still in Africa,*

> Balliol made me, Balliol fed me,
> Whatever I had she gave me again;
> And the best of Blandy
> Balliol loved and led me,
> God be with you, Balliol men.

At one time during his stay at Balliol, Belloc was in lodgings at the former Unicorn Inn on the corner of Blue Boar Street and St Aldate's.

Belloc took British nationality in 1902 and became a Liberal MP in 1906. In a speech to the electorate of South Salford, he announced, 'Gentlemen, I am a Catholic. As far as possible, I go to Mass every day. This is a rosary. As far as possible, I kneel down and tell these beads every day. If you reject me on account of my religion, I shall thank God that He has spared me the indignity of being your representative.' He was elected but, disillusioned with politics, he did not stand for re-election in 1910. He was a close friend of G K Chesterton, who illustrated many of his books. Belloc's *Lines to a Don* are a counterblast to an unwise lecturer's criticism of Chesterton.

Right: Balliol (Hilaire Belloc)

His best known work includes his nonsensical verse for children: *The Bad Child's Book of Beasts* (1896) and the *Cautionary Tales* (1907). From *Cautionary Tales* comes:

> Matilda told such Dreadful Lies,
> It made one Gasp and Stretch one's Eyes;
> Her Aunt, who, from her Earliest Youth,
> Had kept a Strict Regard for Truth,
> Attempted to Believe Matilda:
> The effort very nearly killed her.

In *On His Books* Belloc wrote himself an epitaph:

> When I am dead, I hope it may be said:
> "His sins were scarlet, but his books were read."

John Fothergill

Grasmere-born John Fothergill (1876 to 1957) wrote *An Innkeeper's Diary* which was published in 1931. He went to Bath College and then to St John's College, Oxford where he met Oscar Wilde who was to become a friend. Later Fothergill went to the Slade School of Art. In London, he rubbed shoulders with many beautiful people of the day. Before taking on the Spread Eagle, he ran an art gallery in London.

For a man of Fothergill's background inn keeping was something of an innovation, being considered somewhat *infra.dig.* for a man with any pretensions to gentility. It was his social connections which drew the class of patron that it did and which also enabled him to behave in the fashion of an early Basil Fawlty.

Right: Spread Eagle, Thame

Related in the book are the anecdotes of John Fothergill, pioneer amateur Innkeeper as he described himself, and the sometimes stormy relationship between him and his patrons. Fothergill transformed The Spread Eagle into the first respectable hotel – upsetting dozens of people in the process. The likes of GB Shaw, H G Wells, Evelyn Waugh, G K Chesterton and others stayed there. JIM Stewart, in those days not himself one of the rich and famous, remarks how he and his friends would drive out the 14 or so miles to the Spread Eagle, where Mr Fothergill supplied them with 'a grand sense of *grande cuisine*, with bills to match.'

The stories of his patrons, Fothergill's encounters with local people and his continual battle against those who rushed in to use his toilet without saying please or thank you, made *An Innkeeper's Diary* a runaway best seller that has also been dramatised on television. A blue plaque on the wall of The Spread Eagle commemorates this remarkable man and the 30' tall inn-sign, which caused such a furore when it was first erected, is still very much a feature of the Cornmarket in Thame.

Flora Thompson

Flora Thompson, née Timms, (1876 to 1947) was born in Juniper Hill near Cottisford in the north of the county, on the Northamptonshire border. The first couple of cottages to be built at Juniper Hill were built at a cost of £28 7s 6d in order to house the homeless poor. Two more cottages were added soon afterwards and nothing else for a hundred years until Cottisford Heath was enclosed and several families of squatters and smallholders were re-housed at Juniper Hill so that by the beginning of the 20th century there were 30 cottages in the hamlet.

In *Lark Rise* Flora Thompson relates an old joke about Cottisford being so insignificant that a traveller who asks the way there is

Cottisford church (Flora Thompson)

informed that he has just walked straight through it. Cottisford has no memorial to its most famous inhabitant; her old home remains, as does the school which is now a private house. In the parish church is a war memorial bearing the name of Flora's brother, Edmund Timms. He saw service in the Boer War and in India, then went off to France during the Great War and was killed in France in 1916 when he was 39.

Oxford is only 19 miles to the south geographically, but culturally it was light years away. Flora relates how the majority of the inhabitants of the hamlet had no concept of what Oxford was like, hearing about it only in relation to clergymen and colleges and St Giles' Fair.

One of the hamlet's cottages was Watford Tunnel Cottage where Flora was born, another 'The End House' (re-named 'Larkrise Cottage'), where she spent her childhood. Her father, Albert Timms, worked for 35 years for a builder in Brackley, 3 miles away. Flora went to Cottisford school for seven years and then moved on to work in the post office at Fringford.

Although the trilogy is by definition subjective and was written over half a century after the events described, for anyone interested in the social history of the county in late-Victorian times, it is essential reading. It is the unconscious minor details which make it so authentic. One aspect is the use of the old Oxfordshire speech, for at that time villagers still spoke the local dialect. The vowels were not only broad but often doubled. Flora cites 'boo-oy' for boy, 'pay-ull' for pail and 'brenbu'er' for bread and butter, practices which have not entirely died out. Their conversations were also 'stiff with simile' as she puts it and peppered with proverbs.

The lifestyle of many of the older people of Flora Thompson's world was, in their younger days, not fundamentally very different from that of medieval times, living as they did from hand to mouth, dependent on the weather and the seasons and on the local gentry, which, to a large degree, they still were. In *Lark Rise,* it is made clear that Oxfordshire was a rural county and, as such, badly affected by the agricultural depression of the late-19th century. Poverty and ways to make ends meet are recurrent themes in their Oxfordshire. One amusing example of self-sufficiency is the children's habit of collecting good free food for the pig which the family was fattening up. On wet evenings they would comb the hedgerows for snails which they brought home in a bucket for his supper and which piggy 'crunched up with great relish.'

Flora's writing career started with love stories for women's magazines written to pay for her children's education. These were followed by a series of articles on specific events and characters from her childhood days. Her writings came to the attention of Sir Humphrey Milford of the Oxford University Press who suggested that they be compiled into a book. The semi-autobiographical trilogy, *Lark Rise to Candleford,* appeared between 1939 and 1943. The parts, *Lark Rise (1939), Over to Candleford (1941),* and *Candleford Green*

(1943) were published separately. Flora Thompson also wrote *Still Glides the Stream* (1948), a romance set in Stoke Lyne which she calls 'Fordlow'. It failed to attract the acclaim of her previous work.

Flora left school at 14 to work in the local post office. Many of her contemporaries were far less fortunate as they missed much of their schooling due to their parents keeping them away to earn extra money or to help out with their younger brothers and sisters.

Edward Thomas

(Philip) Edward Thomas (1878 to 1917), who sometimes used the pseudonym Edward Eastaway, was born in London. He took a Second in History in 1900 from Lincoln College and became a hack writer of reviews, critical studies and topographical works. Thomas published a biography of the naturalist Richard Jeffries in 1909 and a novel, *The Happy-Go-Lucky Morgans* in 1913, but it was not until 1914, encouraged by Robert Frost, that he realised his potential as a poet, writing most of his work during active service between 1915 and his death. Thomas enlisted in the Artists' Rifles in 1915 but transferred to the Royal Artillery where he became a Lieutenant. He was killed by an exploding shell at Arras, just before the publication of *Poems* in 1917.

After the war, Edward Thomas's wife, Helen, wrote about their marriage in *As it Was,* which came out in 1926, and *World Without End* in 1931. Their daughter, Myfanwy, published an autobiography, *One of These Fine Days*, in 1982.

John Masefield

John Masefield (1878 to 1967) was born in Ledbury, Herefordshire. The poet and novelist went into the merchant service, where he served his apprenticeship on a sailing ship. Ill health forced him to leave, however, and after three years in New York he returned to England in 1897 and became a journalist. Masefield's earliest and best-known poetical work, *Salt Water Ballads,* includes *Sea Fever.* Masefield was not a member of the University, but received an honorary D Litt at the 1922 Encaenia.

He became Poet Laureate in 1930, a post which he held for 37 years. Masefield lived at Boar's Hill, and his final home in Burcot, near Dorchester, is now the John Masefield Cheshire Home.

Max Beerbohm

(Henry) Max(imilian) Beerbohm (1872 to 1956) blamed his stay at Merton for a personality change, claiming 'I was a 'modest, good-humoured boy. . . It is Oxford that made me insufferable,' and explaining that, 'Undergraduates owe their happiness chiefly to the consciousness that they are no longer at school. The nonsense which was knocked out of them at school is all put gently back at Oxford or Cambridge.'

His best known work, *Zuleika Dobson* (1911), is the story of a young girl visitor to the town who is so beautiful that all the undergraduates commit suicide for love of her by throwing themselves like lemmings into the Isis. *Zuleika Dobson* contains 'A sonnet in Oxfordshire Dialect' which sounds more like a stage Somerset one.

Beerbohm contributed to *The Yellow Book* (1894) and published volumes of caricature, including *Rossetti and His Circle* (1922). He succeeded George Bernard Shaw as critic to the Saturday Review in

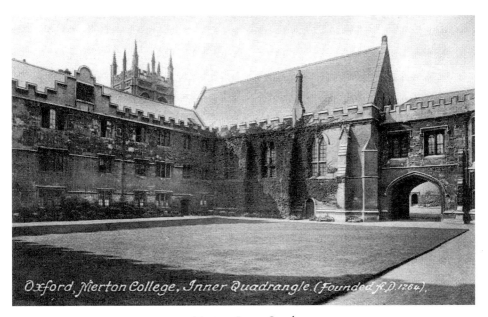

Merton, Inner Quad

1898.

Although he did not proceed to take a degree during his time at Merton and only got a Third in the preliminary Classics Moderations in 1892, he was awarded an honorary D Litt in 1942.

Illustrations from *Zuleika Dobson*, painted by Osbert Lancaster while he was staying at the Randolph Hotel, decorate the walls of the hotel bar and Beerbohm memorabilia can be seen at Merton College.

Lady Otteline Morrell

Lady Otteline Morrell (1873 to1938) was an acknowledged beauty and leading light of the Bloomsbury set. Between the years 1915 and 1924, she was a great patroness of writers, painters, conscientious objectors (her husband having been a pacifist in the Great War), and general freeloaders at their home, 16th-century Garsington Manor. Her husband, Philip, was a lawyer and MP and the Morrells lived at Garsington from 1915 to 1928. Guests were collected from Wheatley station and conveyed to the Manor in style in a carriage sent out from the Manor. Unfortunately, a number of these visitors sneered at the hand that fed them.

Among their regular visitors, the Morrells numbered Katherine Mansfield, Vanessa Bell, Virginia Woolf, Lytton Strachey and Bertrand Russell, her long-time lover. A close friend was DH Lawrence who built the summerhouse and left the manuscript of *The Rainbow* with his hostess when he went to Florida during the obscenity trials. This caused jealousy from his wife, Freida, and, after several unpleasant scenes, the Lawrences moved away to Cornwall. Ottoline must have been dismayed when she found herself portrayed by Lawrence as Hermione in *Women in Love*. Despite the welcome which he received at Garsington Manor and his willingness to hobnob with Oxfordshire society, Lawrence produced poems which announced how beastly he found the bourgeoisie and how he detested what he calls the 'Oxford Voice'. Many of Ottoline's Bloomsbury guests were equally two-faced about their visits to her home.

Ottoline was something of a philanthropist in the village, allowing local schoolchildren to use the manor pool for swimming lessons, established a library in the manor and built a new village hall. The autobiographical *Ottoline at Garsington* which was published in 1974, tells of her years when she played hostess to the great and the not so good of the literary world.

There is a memorial to her in Garsington parish church. The Italianate gardens, which were planned by Ottoline herself, are open through the National Gardens Scheme in early and late summer and are the venue for the Garsington Opera performances between those times.

Sir Winston Churchill

Sir Winston Leonard Spencer Churchill (1874 to 1965) was the son of Lord Randolph Churchill and his American wife. He was born in Blenheim Palace at Woodstock, the seat of his close relative, the Duke of Marlborough. He was premature and happened to born at Blenheim because his mother was attending a party there at the time. His birth room is one of the highlights of a tour of the Palace. In it are treasured some of his clothes and locks of curly hair. Churchill was to say of Blenheim that he took two very important decisions there: to be born and to get married. He proposed to his wife, Clementine, in the Temple of Diana in the Park. He later stated that he was 'happily content with the decision I took on both those occasions.'

Winston Churchill went to Harrow and Sandhurst but not to university. He went into the army for a short while but became a Conservative Member of Parliament in 1900 and held positions in both Liberal and Conservative governments in the early part of the century.

Blenheim Palace (Churchill)

Churchill was Prime Minister from 1940 to 1945 and again from 1951 to 1955, when he resigned office. Nevertheless, he remained an MP until 1964. During the war, he had a weekend headquarters in Oxfordshire at Ditchley Park, near Charlbury. In 1947, he was granted the Freedom of the Borough of Woodstock in a ceremony which took place on the steps of the Town Hall there.

Remembered by the man-in-the-street as a politician and orator, Churchill's first literary works were the campaign reports which he filed from the late-19th century onwards, starting with the South African wars and the Sudan. In 1900, he published his only novel, *Savrola,* and his first major work, the biography of his father, in 1906. Another biography, that of his ancestor, John Churchill, first Duke of Marlborough, followed in four volumes from 1933 to 1938.

His *The World Crisis,* a history of the Great War, came out in 1923–9 followed by his own six-volume memoirs of World War II in 1948–1954. After he gave up office, Churchill set about writing a *History of the English-speaking Peoples* which appeared in four volumes between 1956 and 1958. Many volumes of his wartime speeches have also been published and an autobiography, *My Early Life,* in 1930. Sir Winston Churchill was awarded the Nobel Prize for Literature in 1953.

On his death in 1965, the nation went into a deep mourning that was not to rivalled until the funeral of Princess Diana in 1997. A special train was chartered to bring his body back to Oxfordshire. As the train passed through Oxford, the great bell known as Old Tom, which hangs over the Fair Gate at Christ Church, was tolled. This honour is normally reserved for a Dean of the college or a reigning monarch. The funeral train ended its journey at Long Hanborough station and the cortege continued by road to Bladon, where Churchill is buried alongside several other members of his family in the parish churchyard.

John Buchan

John Buchan (1875 to 1940), later 1st Baron Tweedsmuir, came up to Brasenose from Glasgow University having already had work published. He obtained a First in Classics in 1899, winning the Stanhope Essay prize in 1897 with *Sir Walter Raleigh* and the Newdigate Prize with *The Pilgrim Fathers* the following year. He also won College prizes. In 1934, he was awarded an honorary Doctorate of Civil Law. Buchan must have appreciated the time he spent at Oxford for, in *Memory Hold-the-Door*, he wrote, 'To live for a time close to great minds is the best kind of education.' Of course Buchan's Oxford had greatly improved academically since the time when Hazlitt wrote in *Table Talk*, 'You will hear more good things on the outside of a stagecoach from London to Oxford than if you were to pass a twelvemonth with the undergraduates or heads of colleges of that famous university.'

Of his numerous works, which include the 4-volume *History of the Great War*, the best known is probably *The Thirty-nine Steps*. This novel appeared in 1915 and was made into a film by Sir Alfred Hitchcock in 1935. Other publications include a history of Brasenose College.

Buchan became Member of Parliament for the Scottish Universities in 1927, when he was 52 and created a baron in 1935 when appointed Governor General of Canada by George V. Before he became Lord Tweedsmuir of Elsfield, Buchan lived at Elsfield Manor, just outside Oxford, and his ashes, brought back from Canada, are buried in Elsfield churchyard, under a circular stone.

Joyce Cary

Irishman Joyce Cary (1888 to 1957) came up in 1909 to read Law at Trinity, leaving with a Fourth. At Oxford, he met Gertrude Ogilvie and they married in 1916. Cary had previously trained in art at Edinburgh, but on leaving Oxford pursued neither subject but went off to the Balkans, where he served as a medical orderly for the Red Cross in 1912. After that, Cary joined the colonial service and went out to West Africa, where he spent eight years. He returned to Oxford in 1920, having been wounded while serving with the Nigeria Regiment in the Cameroons, and the Carys lived at 12 Parks Road.

Joyce Cary wrote novels from this time until his death in 1957 and is buried in Wolvercote cemetery.

Compton Mackenzie

Compton Mackenzie (1883 to 1972) was the adopted name of Edward Montague Compton. He was born in West Hartlepool, but saw himself as a Scot. He studied at Oxford at Magdalen College, leaving with a Second in Modern History in 1904 and trained as a lawyer, but gave this up to become a full time writer. The wisdom of this decision was proved by the outstanding success of his first three novels. His semi-autobiographical *Sinister Street* (1913–14) includes Oxford. A later work, *Guy and Pauline* (1915), is a love story set in the English country before the war. At one time Mackenzie lived in a cottage by the Windrush at Burford and the town features in the novel as 'Wychford', a reference to the proximity of Wychwood Forest. The house is mentioned in the Burford Trail as "Ladyham, scene of Compton Mackenzie's novel *Guy and Pauline.*"

Mackenzie's autobiography, *My Life and Times*, appeared in ten volumes between 1963 and 1971. It relates his experiences in the Secret

Service and with the Royal Marines at Gallipoli. During the last years of the war, he was military control officer in Athens, and in 1917 director of the Aegean Intelligence Service. His experiences at that time led to three books: *Gallipoli Memories* (1929), *Athenian Memories* (1931), and *Aegean Memories* (1940). His *Greek Memories* (1932) was withdrawn after his trial under the Official Secrets Act. One of his best-loved works is *Whisky Galore!* which was made into a successful film.

Mackenzie died on St Andrew's Day, 30th November 1972 and was buried at Eoligarry on Barra. During the burial service an old friend played a lament on the bagpipes, then promptly collapsed and died.

Chapter Eight

Thomas Sterns Eliot ✍ *Robert Gibbings* ✍ *Agatha Christie*

J R R Tolkien ✍ *Dorothy L Sayers* ✍ *Vera Brittain*

Aldous Huxley ✍ *Robert Graves* ✍ *Edmund Blunden*

Winifred Holtby ✍ *C S Lewis* ✍ *The Inklings*

Elizabeth Goudge ✍ *George Orwell* ✍ *Evelyn Waugh*

Thomas Sterns Eliot

Thomas Sterns Eliot (1888 to 1965) was born in St Louis, Missouri, and educated at Harvard, the Sorbonne and Merton College. He married and settled in London in 1917 and took British nationality in 1927, the same year that he became an Anglo-Catholic. For a time, Eliot worked in a bank before becoming a lecturer. He then went into publishing with Faber and Faber, where he became a director. Best remembered for *The Waste Land* (1922), *Murder in the Cathedral* (1935) and *Four Quartets* (1944), Eliot won the Nobel Prize for literature in 1948.

Although he did not find his time at Merton an enjoyable experience, Eliot accepted an honorary Doctor of Literature from the University in 1948.

Robert Gibbings

Robert Gibbings (1889 to 1958) was born in Ireland in County Cork, where his father was the rector of Garrettstown and afterwards a canon of St Finbar's Cathedral in Cork City. Gibbings went to University College, Cork, where he enrolled for courses in both medicine and art but left to go to the Slade School in London where he studied in 1911–12. He took up etching and started to design bookplates. In the First World War he enlisted in the Royal Munster Fusiliers and was shot in the neck at Gallipoli in 1915. He returned to Ireland and became a founder member of the Society of Wood Engravers in 1920 and the proprietor of the Golden Cockerel Press between 1924 and 1933. Later, he taught book production at the University of Reading where the Gibbings Archives are held in the Library. A period of travel and the publication of reminiscences followed, culminating in an honorary MA from the University of Ireland in 1938.

The next year Gibbings built a flat bottomed boat which he named the *Willow* and used for exploring the rivers of Britain and Ireland, which resulted in *Sweet Thames Run Softly* in 1940, *Coming Down the Wye* (1942), *Lovely is the Lee*, 1945 and *Sweet Cork of Thee* in 1951.

Sweet Thames Run Softly (its name adapted from one already used by fellow Irishman Edmund Spencer), tells of Gibbings' adventures along the Thames, including Oxfordshire, while *Till I End My Song*, one of his last works and published in 1957, is autobiographical. Robert Gibbings died at Long Wittenham and is buried in the churchyard there.

Agatha Christie

Agatha Christie (1890 to 1976) was born in Torquay in Devon. When the Great War broke out, she worked as a hospital nurse and her first book, published in 1920, *The Mysterious Affair at Styles* (where Torquay is portrayed as Styles), drew on her experiences.

After her husband, Archie Christie, announced that he wanted a divorce, Agatha went missing for a few days. She was staying in a hotel in Harrogate under an assumed name, but the details of her stay remain a mystery.

In the course of her writing career, she produced more than seventy books and among her most famous characters are Hercule Poirot and Miss Marple, the adventures of whom have been made into very successful films and television series. Her *The Mousetrap,* which evolved from the short story, *Three Blind Mice,* is one of the most famous plays of all time. It opened in London in 1952 and on the day that the writer died, 12th January 1976, had its 9612th consecutive performance.

Her second marriage was to the archaeologist Sir Max Mallowan whom she met on an archaeological dig in Iraq. They were married in 1930. Mallowan was himself an Oxford graduate, having taken a Third in *Literae Humaniores* from New College. Agatha Christie is quoted as saying that this was the ideal occupation for a husband, for the older his wife became, the more interested he became in her! They lived for many years at Winterbrook House near Wallingford. She is buried in the churchyard at nearby Cholsey.

J R R Tolkien

John Ronald Reuel Tolkien (1892 to 1973) was born in South Africa but came to England when he was seven.

He came up to Exeter College in 1908, was awarded the College's open Classical Exhibition two years later, took a Second in Classics Moderations in 1913 and a First in English Language and Literature two years later.

After gaining a commission in the Lancashire Fusiliers, he was sent to France in 1916, shortly after his marriage to Edith Bratt. Their son John was born in 1917 and the next year the Tolkiens came back to Oxford to live at 50 St John Street where they stayed until 1918. They then moved to 1 Alfred Street and Tolkien worked on the Oxford English Dictionary project, which at that time was based in the Old Ashmolean Building in Broad Street.

In 1920, he left Oxford to take up a post in the English Department of the University of Leeds where he became Professor of English Language in 1924. This appointment was short lived, for he returned to Oxford in 1925. In that year, he was elected to the prestigious Rawlinson and Bosworth Professorship of Anglo-Saxon at Pembroke College. The family lived at 22 Northmoor Road in North Oxford, but moved next door to number 20 in 1930, a large, grey, detached house which had once been the home of publisher and bookseller, Sir Basil Blackwell, and stayed there for 17 years. Number 20 Northmoor Road has the distinction of being one of only 3 places in Oxford to have blue plaques; the others are 83 High Street where Mrs Cooper made her word-famous Oxford Marmalade and 16 St John Street, once the home of artist William Turner.

In 1937 *The Hobbit*, the companion and forerunner of *The Lord of the Rings* trilogy, was published, followed by *The Fellowship of the Ring* in 1954, *The Two Towers* in 1955 and *The Return of the King* the following year. *The Lord of the Rings,* a saga of the struggle between good and evil in the fantasy land of Middle Earth, was destined to become cult reading in the Sixties and voted as the book of the century in several millennium polls.

In 1945 Tolkien was elected Merton Professor of English Language and Literature and moved from Pembroke to Merton. The family moved to a Merton property, 3 Manor Road, where they lived for three years until they went to 99 Holywell Street which also belonged to Merton.

From 1953 until 1968, the Tolkiens lived at 76 Sandfield Road, Headington, as a plaque above the garage states. Tolkien converted the garage into an office and it is subsequent owners who put the plaque there. Tolkien retired in 1959, and in 1968 they moved to Bournemouth. When Edith died in 1971, however, her husband came back to Oxford and lived in Merton-owned accommodation at 21 Merton Street. In 1972, he was awarded a CBE for his services to literature.

Tolkien himself died in 1973 while in Bournemouth on holiday. He was buried, with Edith, in Wolvercote Cemetery just beyond the Oxford ring road. On the gravestone is the inscription:

EDITH MARY TOLKIEN

LUTHIEN

1889–1971

JOHN RONALD REUEL TOLKIEN

BEREN

1892–1973

In 1992, the centenary of Tolkien's birth, the Tolkien Society and the Mythopoeic Society donated two trees, a silver-leafed maple and a false acacia, which were planted in the University Parks; in addition a bench nearby was put there in his memory.

Tolkien's final work, the *Silmarillion,* edited by his son Christopher, came out in 1977. The £210 million film version (one of the most expensive films made to date) of *The Fellowship of the Ring* came out shortly before Christmas 2001. With a cast which includes Sir Ian McKellan, Sir Ian Holm and Liv Tyler, it was an immediate box office success, winning several Oscars. The second appeared a year afterwards, eventually followed by the third part.

Admirers who wish to visit places associated with the writer are fortunate in that there are more of them than those of any other Oxfordshire writer apart from Lewis Carroll. In addition to his grave, the trees and bench in the Parks and the various houses in which he lived, other Tolkien-related venues are the three Roman Catholic churches which he attended, St Aloysius and St Gregory, both in the Woodstock Road and St Anthony of Padua in Headley Way, Headington; the Eagle and Child public house in St Giles' where the Inklings used to meet; Addison's Walk in the grounds of Magdalen College where he would stroll with CS Lewis and other writers; the Old Ashmolean Building which is now the Museum of the History of Science and open to the public and of course Merton and Pembroke Colleges.

Dorothy L Sayers

Dorothy Leigh Sayers (1893 to 1957) was a native Oxonian, born in Brewer Street just off St Aldate's, where her father was Headmaster of Christ Church Choir School; a plaque on the house, No 1 Brewer Street, marks her birthplace. She took a First in French from Somerville in 1915, but was unable to have her degree conferred for another five years because women were not allowed to do so until 1920. Her first job in publishing was at Blackwell's but she was sacked by Sir Basil Blackwell.

Sayers' best-loved work is the Lord Peter Wimsey whodunit series, set in Oxford; the first of these was *Whose Body?* which appeared in 1923. Another of her novels, *Busman's Honeymoon*, features St Cross church in Holywell. The popular *Gaudy Night* (1935) was filmed recently. In this context, the word 'gaudy' refers to college reunions called gaudies; the word is derived from *gaudere*, the Latin for 'to rejoice.' From this novel comes, 'I admit it is better fun to punt than to

DL Sayers' plaque

be punted, and that a desire to have all the fun is nine-tenths of the law of chivalry.' Perhaps what sums up the supposed romanticism of Oxford for the outsider, is the scene where Wimsey proposes to his girl friend. They are strolling down New College Lane and he asks *'Placetne domina?'* This query is not entirely of Sayers' own invention for *placet or non placet* is used in certain University situations to signify agreement, or the lack of it, when a suggestion is being debated.

In addition to detective fiction, Sayers produced translations of Dante's *Inferno* and *Purgatorio* which were published in 1949 and 1955.

The writer's pertinent comment on 20th-century literature is:

> As I grow older and older,
> And totter towards the tomb,
> I find that I care less and less
> Who goes to bed with whom.

which appeared in *That's Why I Never Read Modern Novels.*

In a review of *The Letters of Dorothy L Sayers,* edited by Barbara Reynolds, in the *Times Literary Supplement,* AN Wilson mentions Sayers' 'desire that everyone should know she was not merely clever, but an Oxford MA led to her wearing an MA gown and one of those grotesque 'penwipers' which women of a certain Oxford generation wore on their heads – not only when attending church, but, sometimes, when going shopping or waddling on to the bus.' The 'penwiper' to which Wilson is referring is the usually unflattering choir-girl style soft cap which has largely been replaced by the mortar board as part of both men's and women's academic dress.

Vera Brittain

Vera Brittain (1893 to 1970) was born at Newcastle under Lyme, Staffordshire, the daughter of a successful paper manufacturer. When Vera decided that she wanted to go to Somerville College, where she had gained a type of scholarship known as an Exhibition, her father opposed the idea initially, but finally agreed to it. Unfortunately, when she did come up to Oxford, her first year at Oxford was spoiled by the shadow of the war which hung over young people of her generation.

The first part of her autobiography, *Testament of Youth* (1933), is a story of 'the lost generation' and the changes brought about by the Great War. The subject matter is similar to that of Robert Graves's autobiography *Goodbye to All That* which had already appeared in 1929. Although the treatment differs, both books deal with the loss of a life-style which had vanished for ever.

In *Testament of Youth,* Brittain relates how, when Somerville was requisitioned during the war, its inmates were moved to Oriel College and lodged in St Mary Quad on the site of the former St Mary Hall. Where the female students were accommodated was, of course, walled off from the exclusively male residents of Oriel proper. However, these

Oriel, St Mary Quad (Vera Brittain)

gentlemen 'concluded that it would be a first-rate 'rag' to break down the wall which divided them from the carefully guarded young females in St Mary Hall. Great perturbation filled the souls of the Somerville dons when they came down to breakfast one morning to find that a large gap had suddenly appeared in the protecting masonry, through which had been thrust a hilarious placard: 'OO MADE THIS 'ERE 'OLE?'

'MICE!!!'

Throughout that day and the following night the Senior Common Room, from the Principal downwards, took it in turns to sit on guard beside the hole, for fear any unruly spirit should escape through it to the forbidden, adventurous males on the other side.'

During the War Vera Brittain left Somerville temporarily and served as a Voluntary Aid Detachment nurse. Her fiancé, Roland Leighton, was killed by a sniper's bullet in 1915. She also lost her younger brother Edward, who died in 1918 on the Italian Front, and two close friends, Geoffrey Thurlow and Victor Nicholson. Their moving correspondence, *Letters From A Lost Generation*, was published in 1999.

Brittain worked as a nurses' aide in hospitals in Malta and near the Western Front, nursing English soldiers and German prisoners, and witnessing firsthand the consequences of battle. These experiences turned Brittain into a confirmed pacifist, and an active member of peace movements in both England and the United States.

After the war, she worked as a teacher in Oxford and in 1922 moved to London, devoting herself to writing. Between the years 1921 and 1925, Brittain travelled extensively in Europe. Her journeys included visits to the Rhineland, the Ruhr, and Cologne, during the post-war occupation of Germany.

Vera developed a close friendship with the novelist and ardent feminist Winifred Holtby (1898–1935), the author of *South Riding*, whom she had met at Oxford.

In 1923, Brittain published her first novel, *The Dark Tide*. This deals with the time she spent at Somerville and the problems of being a woman in the man's world of Oxford. Its heroines, Virginia Dennison and Daphne Lethbridge, are recognisable as Vera Brittain and Winifred Holtby. The novel was badly received in Oxford, where academics protested that it showed the University in an unfavourable light.

Apart from *Testament of Youth* and its sequel, *Testament of Experience*, Vera Brittain wrote *Testament of Friendship* which was published in 1940 as a memorial to Winifred Holtby.

Vera Brittain died in London on March 29, 1970. Her daughter, Shirley Williams, also a member of Somerville College, was a prominent Labour Party politician and cabinet minister. She co-founded the Social Democratic Party in 1981.

Aldous Huxley

Aldous Huxley (1894 to 1963) was the son of TH Huxley and brother of Julian Huxley, both of whom were distinguished biologists. Through his mother's family, he was related to Matthew and Thomas Arnold. Aldous won a scholarship to Eton in 1908, but after a short time there he was forced to leave because of a serious eye infection which left him almost blind.

He had to learn braille and be taught at home by a tutor, but finally his eyesight improved sufficiently for him to come up to Balliol to read English from 1913 to 1916. While he was at Oxford, he came into contact with such lions as Bertrand Russell and also DH Lawrence with whom he struck up a close friendship. Lawrence, who had no connections with the University himself, wrote a poem in which he expresses his dislike of the Oxford accent. Nevertheless, he concealed it sufficiently to take part in the social gatherings of writers and artists at Garsington Manor where they were guests of Lady Ottoline Morrell. Huxley's major work, *Brave New World,* was published in 1931.

In the Thirties, Huxley took his family to California where he worked as a screenwriter. He died on the day that JF Kennedy was assassinated, 22nd November 1963.

Robert Graves

Robert Ranke Graves (1895 to 1985) was born in London. During World War I, he served with the Royal Welch Fusiliers, in the same regiment as the writer and poet Siegfried Sassoon. In 1919, after the War, Graves came up to St John's and received a dispensation to live at Boar's Hill, some five miles outside the city, due to his lungs which had suffered as a result of the War. He obtained a Third in Classics

Moderations in 1923 and Third in Classics two years later. In 1926, he was Professor of English in Cairo.

Graves established his reputation with *Good-bye to All That* (1929), an outspoken book on his war experiences which includes the effect which the war had on the little community of Boar's Hill. With his wife, he opened a shop there and operated a sliding scale of charges, with the better-off customers paying more than the less wealthy.

A versatile and highly prolific writer, Graves thought of himself primarily as a poet, but he is best known for his unorthodox novels of Roman history, *I, Claudius* (1934) and *Claudius the God* (1934), both of which were successfully adapted for television, as well as fictionalised versions of history and myth such as *King Jesus* (1946).

In addition to *Wife to Mr Milton*, Graves' novel on the life of Marie Powell, John Milton's young wife, another Oxford subject is the General Elliott pub in Manor Road, South Hinksey. In 1920, Graves wrote a poem about both pub and landlord. The General himself became famous for having defended Gibraltar against Spanish attack from 1779 to 1793 and was created Baron Heathfield.

Graves moved to Majorca before it became overrun with tourists. He lived in Mallorca for the next few years and ran the Seizin Press in partnership with the American writer Laura Riding, and after World War II he went back to the island.

Robert Graves was Professor of Poetry at Oxford from 1961 to 1966. He also lived at Islip and spent the latter part of his life at Boar's Hill.

Edmund Blunden

Edmund Charles Blunden (1896 to 1974) was born in London but soon afterwards moved to Kent. He went to school at Christ's Hospital and then went on to the Queen's College, Oxford. During the Great War, Blunden held a commission in the Royal Sussex Regiment and saw active service in France and Belgium from 1916 to 1919, both on the Somme and at Ypres. He was awarded the Military Cross for his bravery.

Blunden's collection of poems entitled *The Waggoner* appeared in 1920, aided by Siegfried Sassoon who was then Literary Editor of *The Daily Herald*. This was the start of a friendship which would last a lifetime. Blunden's account of the First World War appeared in 1928 as *Undertones of War* and won him considerable acclaim. This was enforced by *The Poems of Edmund Blunden* published in 1930.

Unfortunately for Blunden, his work has since been overshadowed by that of other war poets, notably Sassoon himself and Wilfred Owen, the edition of whose poetry was published in 1931 by Blunden and aroused longstanding public interest. Blunden also wrote about the English countryside, his subject matter being similar to that of Hardy and Housman.

Between the Wars Blunden worked as a literary journalist and held the post of Professor of English Literature at the University of Tokyo from 1924 to 1927. On his return to England he became Fellow and tutor in English at Merton College where he stayed from 1931 to 1943, leaving Oxford to work for the *Times Literary Supplement* before returning to Tokyo in 1948 with the UK Liaison Mission. The year 1950 saw him back with the *TLS* before being appointed Emeritus Professor of English Literature at Hong Kong University in 1953. The Queen's Gold medal for poetry followed in 1956 and a return to England early in the next decade.

Blunden was elected Professor of Poetry at Oxford in 1966 but only served two years in office, being forced to resign on the grounds of ill health. His last years were spent with his third wife and four children in Suffolk at Long Melford, where, in 1966, he wrote a guide to the fine parish church.

Winifred Holtby

Winifred Holtby (1898 to 1935) was born in Rudston, Yorkshire, the daughter of David Holtby, a farmer, and Alice Winn, the first woman alderman on the East Riding County Council. It was Alice who encouraged Winifred to write poetry and arranged for her daughter's first collection of poems to appear in print when she was only 13.

Winifred came up to Somerville College in 1917, but, like her close friend Vera Brittain, left Oxford for a time to work in a nursing home in London and as a volunteer in the Signal Unit of the Women's Auxiliary Corps. She was sent to France in 1918 and came back to Oxford the following year to finish her degree in history.

After graduating with a Second in 1921, Winifred worked as a journalist on the *Manchester Guardian,* the *Daily Express,* the *Evening Standard, Good Housekeeping*, and the *News Chronicle.*

Holtby, Brittain and a tortoise shared a flat in London. The two women kept in touch throughout their adult lives and Winifred Holtby's correspondence with Vera Brittain was published as *Letters to a Friend* in 1937.

Unfortunately, Winifred suffered from a heart condition, which gradually weakened her and, when she collapsed in 1932, she was told that she was exhausted from working too hard. After this happened again Bright's disease (one which affects the kidneys) was diagnosed. She died in September 1935, having managed to finish her novel *South Riding* which was published with the assistance of Vera Brittain who was her literary executor. *South Riding* won the 1936 James Tait Black Memorial Prize.

C S Lewis

Born in Ulster in 1898, Clive Staples Lewis came up to University College in 1916. He got a First Class in Literae Humaniores in 1922 and in 1925 became a Fellow of Magdalen College where he had rooms in the New Buldings. In 1998, a commemorative plaque was unveiled in Addison's Walk where Lewis used to stroll in the college grounds. To mark the centenary of Lewis's birth, a stone was inscribed with a poem which he wrote describing his walks along the riverbank.

He shared a house in Headington Quarry, with his brother, Warnie. During his time at Oxford, he wrote *The Allegory of Love* in 1936, followed by *The Screwtape Letters* in 1942. From 1954 to 1963, Lewis held a professorship at Cambridge and published works on 16th-century English Literature. He is best known, perhaps, for the *Narnia* series of books which appeared between 1948 and 1956. Lewis's popularity with his wider audience was not shared by his Oxford colleagues. It has been suggested that his fellow academics were jealous of his success, but reminiscences of those who came into contact with Lewis on a day-to-day basis indicate that they found him a less than attractive personality.

In 1956 he married the American writer Joy Gresham and it is this relationship which led to Lewis's autobiographical *Surprised by Joy* of 1955 and *Shadowlands*, which started off as a play and was turned into a film. This was directed by Sir Richard Attenborough in 1993 at venues such as the Sheldonian Theatre and Magdalen College itself.

CS Lewis died in 1963, on 22nd November (the same day as Aldous Huxley), and is buried in the churchyard of Holy Trinity church in Headington Quarry. He is commemorated by the Study Centre run by the CS Lewis Foundation at 'The Kilns', his home for 33 years; nearby is the CS Lewis Nature reserve. The Foundation bought The Kilns, in Lewis Close, Risinghurst on the eastern edges of Oxford in the 1980s

Right: CS Lewis's grave

for £130,000 and restored it to how it would have looked fifty years previously.

The CS Lewis Foundation, backed by English Heritage, attempted to obtain listed status for 'The Kilns' in a move to protect it from any future proposed development or demolition. In February 2002, however, the Department of Culture, Media and Sport turned down the application on the grounds that the bungalow was not of sufficient architectural merit, being a small redbrick bungalow on the edge of a housing estate. At the time of writing, the CS Lewis Foundation allows members of the public to take tours of The Kilns.

Although the Lewises are principally associated with The Kilns, CS Lewis in fact lived in two other houses in Headington. The first is 'Uplands', 54 Windmill Road (before which he lived at 28 Warneford Road, off Divinity Road); then he lodged at 'Hillsboro', 14 Holyoake Road, off the main London Road. In the 1920s, Lewis lodged there with a lady named Mrs Janie Moore and in 1930 they both moved to 'The Kilns' which was owned jointly by Mrs Moore and the Lewis brothers. Mrs Moore died in January 1951 and is buried in Holy Trinity churchyard along with CS Lewis.

Yet another Headington connection is 10 Old High Street which Lewis helped Joy Davidman to rent; also known by her original married name of Joy Gresham, she was later to become Mrs Lewis.

The Inklings

The Inklings literary group dates back to the 1930s when it was formed as a literary society by an undergraduate member of University College. The society encouraged members to present their unpublished literary efforts. After the founder left Oxford, the club

Right: Eagle and Child (The Inklings)

continued to flourish around a nucleus formed by CS Lewis, Tolkien and Nevill Coghill. Also included were Lewis's brother, Major Warren Lewis, Charles Williams (who is buried in Holywell Cemetery) and RE Harvard who was Lewis's and Tolkien's doctor. They met regularly on weekday mornings, in the Bird and Baby, properly the Eagle and Child public house in St Giles'. The Thursday evening gatherings were accompanied by tea and pipe tobacco in CS Lewis's rooms at Magdalen. The Inklings continued to meet throughout the war years and into the 1950s. Admirers of this group of writers make pilgrimages to the Eagle and Child where Inkling memorabilia can be seen.

Elizabeth Goudge

Elizabeth Goudge (1900 to 1984) was born in Wells, the daughter of Dr Henry Leighton Goudge. She lived for a time at Christ Church where her father was Regius Professor of Divinity from 1923 to 1939.

Chapter IX of Elizabeth Goudge's autobiography, *The Joy of the Snow*, which was published in 1974, is entitled 'Oxford'. In it, she describes the Goudge family's arrival at Oxford in their new home in Tom Quad overlooking the Mercury fountain. Their house was long and narrow, with a dining room where portraits of divines who had died in the house stared haughtily down from the walls. Elizabeth Goudge says that no one seemed to have actually lived as opposed to died in their new home. It had no atmosphere, good or bad, and did not even possess a ghost! Unable to feel any empathy with the house, Elizabeth would roam round Oxford and the surrounding countryside, while her father went about his academic business and her invalid mother kept herself occupied with the garden at the rear of the house.

Elizabeth's chief memories of Oxford are spotting kingfishers in

Christ Church Meadow, finding bluebells in Bagley Wood near Kennington, the ancient library at Merton, the stair case leading up to Christ Church Hall, New College garden which includes a stretch of the city wall, and Magdalen cloisters. 'Those cloisters were for me the heart of Oxford,' she writes.

Also concerning cloisters, she quotes a limerick by Monsignor Ronald Knox:

> There was once a man who said 'God
> Must think it exceedingly odd
> If he finds that this tree
> Continues to be
> When there's no one about in the Quad.'

with the anonymous reply:

> 'Dear Sir, Your astonishment's odd:
> *I* am always about in the Quad.
> And that's why the tree
> Will continue to be,
> Since observed by Yours faithfully, God.'

Knox was one of the numerous Oxford characters who were so fascinating to the newcomer. There was also Warden Spooner of New College, who, she writes, sometimes deliberately made up Spoonerisms which he could be noted hatching before he was due to make a speech.

The family, in particular Elizabeth's father, were well aware of the slum districts of Oxford, some of which lay not far from the grandeur of Christ Church. This disparity between the privileged and the poverty-stricken made her father bad tempered and restless so that he felt angry with those responsible, some of whom were the colleges themselves as landlords.

Everyday life in a college was not entirely without its drawbacks.

Christ Church, Tom Quad (Elizabeth Goudge)

One of the worst of these was the spectacle of noisy students getting rid of surplus energy. Night after night they would be out in Tom Quad blowing hunting horns and cracking whips in the moonlight. Next day they would come round and apologise in a most charming manner to those whose windows they had broken during their nocturnal activities.

Elizabeth Goudge's novel *Towers in the Mist* is the story of the Leigh family who, like her own, lived in one of the Canons' houses in Tom Quad, but in Elizabethan times. Another, *The White Witch* (1958) is set in the Chiltern Hills above Henley-on-Thames and in Oxford itself, during the Civil War. In the 1970s, Elizabeth Goudge herself lived at Rose Cottage in Dog Lane on the outskirts of Henley, the inspiration for the cottage of the gypsy Froniga in *The White Witch*. When she first moved to Rose Cottage in the 1950s, Elizabeth saw Froniga come through the hedge. Then she disappeared before the author's eyes and was never seen by her again.

The writer stayed on in Rose Cottage, but during the early 1990s a fire ruined the cottage and renovations changed its character. In 2000, the cottage was sold with a view to modernisation. The purchaser has been quoted as saying that he had never heard of Elizabeth Goudge, let alone Froniga, the White Witch.

In *The White Witch* the hero, Robert Haslewood, has been to Thame Grammar School with Hampden, while the Haslewood family go into Henley, four miles away from their manor house. There is a description of the town as the King's horsemen clatter along Bell Street and into Hart Street. As a trusted Parliamentarian, Robert attends secret meetings at Broughton Castle in the north of Oxfordshire, near Banbury.

Some of Elizabeth's favourite places feature in the book: Christ Church Meadow, Merton and New College cloisters, peopled by members of Charles I's Court who were living there during the Civil War. Other places mentioned in the book are right away from the tourist trail, like the wooded plain of Shotover, St Bartholomew's Chapel off the Cowley Road which was once a leper hospital, and St Margaret's well at Binsey which so fascinated Lewis Carroll.

In *The Scent of Water* (1963), also set in the Henley area but in the mid-20th century, Mary, the central character, is left a decrepit cottage in Appleshaw, a tiny village among the beech woods of the Chiltern Hills. Westwater, 'a country town by the river which was the nearest shopping-place of any size' is obviously modelled on Henley.

George Orwell

George Orwell (1903 to 1950), whose real name was Eric Blair, is buried in Sutton Courtenay churchyard. After leaving Eton in 1921, he returned to his native India to join the Imperial Police, but six years later came back to England. He adopted the pen name George Orwell for the publication of his first book, *Down and Out in Paris and London,* in 1933.

After a successful period of writing, he went off to Spain in 1936, only to be wounded in the neck and return to England in 1938. However, he developed tuberculosis which he foolishly neglected. His *Animal Farm* earned him instant acclaim, but Blair evaded fame and fortune by moving to the Scottish island of Jura. This only worsened his tubercular condition, and after writing his most famous novel, *1984,* he moved back to England. By this time, the disease had taken a serious hold on him and he died in January 1950.

Blair specifically requested that he be buried, according to rites of the Anglican Church, in an English country churchyard. The Astor family owned the manor of Sutton Courtenay and David Astor was a friend of Orwell for many years as well as his boss on the *Observer* newspaper. Astor was in a position to be able to arrange for Blair to be buried in everyone's idea of an English country village.

Evelyn Waugh

Born in London, Evelyn Waugh (1903 to 1966) took a Third in Modern History from Hertford College in 1924. Waugh soon acquired fame with the publication of novels of the calibre of *Decline and Fall* (1928), *Vile Bodies* (1930), and *Scoop* (1938). He became a Catholic in 1930 and his later books are of a more serious nature, as in *Brideshead Revisited* (1945), a nostalgic evocation of student days at Oxford, which also explores Catholicism and was made into a successful television series. Waugh captures the atmosphere of an Oxford Sunday away from the tourist trails where 'None but church-goers seemed abroad,' in 'half a dozen conflicting sects; on their way to St Barnabas, St Columba, St Aloysius, St Mary's, Pusey House . . . '

Despite its being considered one of the leading 'Oxford' novels and being used as an adjective, little of *Brideshead* is in fact set in Oxford. Only Chapters One and Five of Book One, *Et in Arcadia Ego,* contain Oxford scenes.

One of the heroes, Sebastian Flyte, occupies a set of rooms in Christ Church's Meadow Buildings. The other, Charles Ryder, is at one of the smaller colleges which is generally taken to be Waugh's own Hertford. For a period, less conscientious guides showed tourists the spot where, in the novel, Flyte is sick through Ryder's open ground floor window.

Waugh spent his honeymoon in 1928, and subsequently when he was writing *Dante Gabriel Rossetti,* at the Abingdon Arms in Beckley, one of the 'towns' of Otmoor. Beckley Park features as the country house which is the setting for Aldous Huxley's *Crome Yellow;* the descriptions of the activities of the residents and their guests were suggested by those of Garsington Manor.

Chapter Nine

Nancy Mitford ✍ *Unity Mitford* ✍ *Jessica Mitford*

Graham Greene ✍ *Anthony Powell* ✍ *John Betjeman*

JIM Stewart ✍ *W H Auden* ✍ *Louis MacNeice*

William Golding ✍ *Mollie Harris* ✍ *Barbara Pym* ✍ *Miss Read*

Dylan Thomas

Nancy Mitford

Nancy Mitford (1904 to 1973) was the eldest of the one son and six daughters of Lord Redesdale who owned houses at both Astall and Swinbrook in the Oxfordshire Cotswolds. The family moved to Astall in 1919 before moving on to Swinbrook where the house was built by Redesdale in 1927. The children, however, hated the house, complaining that it was cold, bare and unwelcoming.

Nancy's *Love in a Cold Climate* (1949), was made into a film for television shot locally and this novel, as well as *The Pursuit of Love* (1945), tells of life in the family homes, Astall Manor and Swinbrook House and features both Swinbrook and the adjoining village of Astall.

Nancy was born in London and worked as the manager of a London bookshop during the War, then moved to Paris in 1945. She was a journalist and biographer and a close friend of Evelyn Waugh who criticised her unconventional writing style. Because of her left-wing tendencies, Nancy caused a rift in the aristocratic Mitford family, the members of which did not all appreciate her satirical treatment of the

Establishment. The main legacy from these works is the concept of something being 'U' or non-U', that is socially acceptable or not. Besides novels and lively correspondence with her sisters and Waugh, Nancy Mitford wrote historical biographies of a high standard, notably of Madame de Pompadour (1954) and Frederick the Great (1970).

In 1967, Nancy moved to a house in Versailles which coincided with the onset of a long period of illness which finally turned out to be Hodgkin's Disease. Nancy never came back to England but died in France in June 1973. She was cremated in the Père Lachaise cemetery in Paris and her ashes returned to be buried in Swinbrook churchyard near her sister Unity who had died in 1948. Nancy, who professed a dislike of crosses, has a hedgehog on her memorial stone.

Unity Mitford

Unity Mitford, who, through their brother-in-law, the British fascist leader Sir Oswald Moseley, met members of the German National Socialist party, became a great admirer of Hitler, and was admitted to his circle of friends. When, during a visit to Germany, Unity learned that Britain had declared war on September 3, 1939, she attempted to commit suicide by shooting herself. She pulled through, thanks to the attentions of Hitler's medical men, and returned home to England.

Jessica Mitford

Jessica Mitford (1917 to 1996), the younger sister of Nancy and Unity, became known for her books on controversial social and political issues. In 1937, she made headlines by running off to Spain with

Esmond Romilly (a nephew of Winston Churchill), who had joined the International Brigade to fight General Franco. The couple moved to the United States in 1939, but Romilly was killed in action in World War II in 1941 while on active service with the Canadian Air Force.

After marrying her second husband, the lawyer Robert Treuhaft, in 1943, Jessica took American nationality and in 1960 she published an autobiography of her early life called *Daughters and Rebels*; a second, *A Fine Old Conflict,* which charted her political activities, appeared in 1977. Other works were *The American Way of Death* (1963), *The Trial of Dr. Spock* (1969), *Kind and Unusual Punishment: The Prison Business* (1973) and *The American Way of Birth* (1992). At the time of her death, she was working on a new edition of *The American Way of Death.*

Graham Greene

Graham Greene (1904 to 1991) was born in Berkhamsted, Hertfordshire. He took a Second in Modern History from Balliol in 1925 and received an Honorary D Litt in 1979.

During his time at Oxford, Greene converted to Catholicism. Later he moved to London, where he became a journalist and then a freelance writer. His early novels, beginning with *The Man Within* (1929) and entertaining ones such as *Stamboul Train* (1932), are like thrillers in their approach. His major novels deal with religious issues, first in *Brighton Rock* (1938), and then in *The Power and the Glory* (1940*), The End of the Affair* (1951), and *A Burnt-Out Case* (1961).

Greene also wrote several plays, film scripts (*The Third Man,* 1949), short stories, and essays, as well as three volumes of autobiography. He lived in Antibes for many years until his death in 1991.

Anthony Powell

Anthony Powell (1905 to 2000) was born in Westminster and went to Eton College. From there he went on to read Modern History at Balliol College from 1923 to 1926 and left with a Third. The same year he joined the publishers Duckworth where he rose to become an editor and had his first book *The Bernard Letters* published. In 1939, after a series of jobs, he took a commission in the Welch Regiment and rose to the rank of Major, being demobbed in 1945. The following year he completed his work on John Aubrey which he had started before the outbreak of war.

In 1951 came the first novel in the *A Dance to the Music of Time* series, *A Question of Upbringing,* and two years later he became Literary Editor of *Punch.* He was to write a most informative Introduction to the Oxford University Press's paperback edition of Cuthbert Bede's *The Adventures of Mr Verdant Green.*

In 1971 he was awarded an honorary D Litt by the University of Sussex and two years later Powell was offered a knighthood by the then Prime Minister and fellow Balliolensis, Edward Heath. This he declined. In his *Journals 1987–1989,* under Friday 13 November 1987, the day he was offered the Companion of Honour, Powell wrote that he felt a knighthood to be 'undesirable for a writer', although why this should be the case has never been established. He did, however, accept an honorary Fellowship of his old college in 1974, the year that the 11th volume of *Dance, Temporary Kings,* was awarded the WH Smith Literary Prize, and he received a DLitt from Oxford in 1980.

The poem *Iron Aspidistra* was written by one-time Professor of Poetry Roy Fuller as a tribute to Anthony Powell on his 80th birthday. It was published in a limited edition of 400 in 1985 by the Sycamore Press, Oxford and is a spoof work, supposedly written by the author Mark Members, a character in *A Dance to the Music of Time.*

Anthony Powell died at his home, The Chantry, near Frome in Somerset, in 2000.

John Betjeman

John Betjeman (1906 to 1984) was born in London, near Highgate. The family name was originally Betjemann, but John dropped the second 'n' during the First World War, to make the name look less Germanic.

He was an only child, one of his closest companions being his teddy bear, Archibald, who was to be the star of his children's tale, *Archie and the Strict Baptists*. In the story, Archie lives up on the Downs but pays regular flying visits to Wantage to attend Baptist meetings, using brown paper wings of his own making. At the age of eleven, John became a boarder at the Dragon School in Oxford and three years later he went on to Marlborough College.

In 1925, Betjeman went to Magdalen College, where he was one of CS Lewis's students. Although the two men were totally different in personality and outlook, when describing his own Oxford days, Betjeman writes admiringly of Lewis, calling him, 'Breezy, tweedy, beer-drinking and jolly.' It was for these reasons that he was popular with 'extrovert undergraduates.'

In Betjeman's time, as in Wilde's, junior members were still largely divided into hearties and aesthetes, both parties being illustrated in his book *An Oxford University Chest*. The writer himself was, naturally enough, an aesthete, with colourful, fashionable clothes, long hair and a contempt for playing fields and sports of any kind. The aesthetes never ate in college halls but patronised restaurants, in particular the George, on the corner of George Street and Cornmarket. Many people dined in their sets of college rooms.

Sherry parties were also very much in vogue, not always of the most genteel kind as they could lead to anti-social behaviour such as spitting on passers-by from the top of St Mary Magdalen church tower. On one occasion, when the young offenders came down to ground level, they were met by the Proctors and fined.

Although Betjeman's own college, Magdalen, enjoyed a certain reputation from having had Edward VII as a member while he was

St Mary Magdalen (John Betjeman)

Prince of Wales, the writer cites Balliol ('Scottish and Frugal') as the most academic, and Christ Church as the best college socially. Most of its members had blue blood and there were many instances of Gentlemen of the House throwing out existing furnishings from their rooms in order to carry out an entire redecoration programme. Betjeman's best friend at Christ Church was 'a tow-haired boy from Gresham's' called Wystan Auden.

Having failed a divinity exam, Betjeman did not complete his degree and left Oxford in 1928. This disaster features in *Summoned by Bells* as the termination of what the writer had seen as an idyll which would last his lifetime. He was given a reference by CS Lewis for use while applying for posts as a private schoolteacher, but it was so 'double-edged that I withdrew it after my first unsuccessful application for a post.' He eventually did become a teacher before working as a private secretary, and then going on to teaching at another preparatory school.

In 1931 his first book of poems, *Mount Zion*, was published by an old Oxford friend, Edward James. Soon afterwards, he met and married Penelope Chetwode, the daughter of Field Marshal Lord Chetwode, a former Commander-in-Chief in India.

The Betjemans set up home in Uffington where they lived at Garrards Farm in 1934. They quickly became involved in village life there, John being people's churchwarden and Penelope a director of amateur dramatics and a member of the Women's Institute. John would travel up to London by train, in those days there being stations at both Uffington and Challow.

The family expanded to include their son Paul who was born at Uffington. Their daughter Candida was born in 1942, during their sojourn in Ireland when John was Press Attache to the British Ambassador there. They returned to Uffington the following year, but moved in 1945 to the Old Rectory at Farnborough, over the border in Berkshire. *Archie and the Strict Baptists* is an account of the move. There the Betjemans continued to enjoy a lifestyle similar to the one they had known at Uffington.

They moved back to Oxfordshire in 1951 to live at The Mead in Wantage where they stayed for more than twenty years. John described their home, 'this house is an ugly little thing in a lovely setting of apple trees and meadows by a mill stream right in the centre of Wantage.'

By the mid Fifties, Betjeman had become well known for his radio and television appearances featuring architecture and campaigning for many buildings threatened with demolition.

Summoned by Bells, his autobiography in verse, contains many references to places in Oxfordshire. Betjeman writes about evocative, but everyday, Oxford things: lace curtains and potted plants, churches and bells, tea and toast, bicycles and books, youth and age, Summertown and Jericho. One of his passions was the Oxford Preservation Trust; he cared deeply for the conservation of old buildings and worked tirelessly for this cause, not only in Oxford but throughout the area.

John Betjeman's broadcasting career continued throughout the Sixties and Seventies, with documentaries such as *Metroland* and *A Passion for Churches*. In 1969, he was knighted, and when Cecil Day Lewis died in 1972, he was made Poet Laureate.

Meanwhile, Penelope Betjeman ran the tea rooms known as King Alfred's Kitchen in Wantage's Newbury Street and became involved with the church. The cafe gained notoriety as being the town's first venue to boast an espresso coffee machine and attracting bikers.

The Betjemans left Oxfordshire for Cornwall in 1972 and he wrote a poem to mark the event entitled *On Leaving Wantage, 1972,* in which he mentions the pleasure he got from living in the town. The Poet's Walk runs along Letcombe Brook and through the John Betjeman Millennium Park.

John's last book of new poems, *A Nip in The Air*, was published two years afterwards. After that, he began to suffer from Parkinson's Disease, then a series of strokes. His last appearance in public was at St Pancras Station when he christened a locomotive named after him.

John Betjeman died on May 19th 1984, at his home in Cornwall at Trebetherick, where he had spent many happy childhood holidays. He is buried there in St Enodoc's churchyard.

JIM Stewart

JIM Stewart (1906 to 1994) also wrote under the name of Michael Innes. John Innes Macintosh Stewart was born in Edinburgh. He came up to Oriel College in 1925, shortly after his nineteenth birthday, where he took a First in English in 1928. He states that, in his time at the college, very little had changed since the turn of the century, despite the War to end all Wars.

He would set off on Sunday walks with the Provost of Oriel 'for a chat with the tramps' at Headington Workhouse, as Provost Phelps was much interested in vagrancy, having been a member of the Poor Law Commission of 1905–1909. In the course of their outings, Dr Phelps regaled his undergraduate companion with what were supposed to be memoirs of Matthew Arnold and John Henry Newman, both of whom were Orielenses.

Ironically, Stewart won the Matthew Arnold Memorial Prize in 1929 and was named a Bishop Frazer's scholar. In 1929, after graduating, he went off to Vienna where he studied Freudian psychoanalysis for a year. The scholarship of Stewart's first book, an edition of Florio's translation of Montaigne, earned him a lectureship at the University of Leeds (1930–1935).

From 1936, Stewart was a professor of English at the University of Adelaide, in South Australia. While en route from Liverpool to Adelaide, Stewart wrote his first mystery story, *Death at the President's Lodging* (1936). He spent two years at Queen's University in Belfast. In 1949, he was appointed Student of Christ Church, Oxford, twenty years after he had left Oriel. This was at the end of another war and one which had made a great difference to the place, notably by forcing up academic standards. From 1969 to 1973, Stewart also held the position of University Reader in English Literature.

Stewart had a successful career both as a scholar and a novelist. He first began writing mystery novels in the 1930s, using the pseudonym Michael Innes, and over the next half-century published biographies of Hardy and Kipling which were very well received, as well as five other volumes of literary history and criticism, four volumes of short stories, twenty-two novels which appeared under his own name and in excess of fifty novels which he wrote as Michael Innes. The thriller, *Operation Pax*, published in 1951, includes a chase set in the miles of shelving of the Bodleian Library.

Stewart also wrote many reviews for the *Times Literary Supplement* and other periodicals, in addition to works for the radio. His autobiography is called *Michael Innes and Me: A Memoir.* JIM Stewart wrote a sequence of novels in the manner of Anthony Powell's *Dance to the Music of Time*, called *A Staircase in Surrey;* in this case, Surrey is a college, not a county. This series consisted of *The Gaudy* (1975), *Young Pattullo* (1976), *A Memorial Service* (1976), *The Madonna of the Astrolabe* (1977) and *Full Term* (1979).

W H Auden

Wystan Hugh Auden (1907 to 1973) was an undergraduate at Christ Church where he took a Third in English in 1928. Despite this disappointing result, years later he was elected Professor of Poetry from 1956 to 1960.

All that time ago, Auden found that 'Oxford city is sheer hell. Compared with New York it's five times as crowded and the noise of the traffic is six times louder. Ironically enough, I had to leave New

Christ Church with Brew House (WH Auden)

York and come to Oxford in order to get robbed.'

In his later years he was allowed to live in the Brewhouse in the grounds of Christ Church in which to end his days, and there is a memorial in the cathedral which marks the pew to which he would come to services in his slippers. Auden used to cross the road from his cottage to St Aldate's Coffee House where he held court, surrounded by young hopefuls, Auden chain-smoking throughout. One of this Coffee House circle (also known as The Gang), was Cecil Day Lewis, then at Wadham. After taking his degree, Day Lewis taught at Summer Fields School in North Oxford, where he lived above the lodge. He adopted the pen name Nicholas Blake for writing a novel about his experiences. He also wrote poetry and detective stories. Day Lewis was himself Professor of Poetry from 1951 to 1955. Philip Larkin wrote that Auden's was 'An engaging, bookish, American talent, too verbose to be memorable and too intellectual to be moving.'

Auden was given an honorary D Litt 1971. On 4th October 1973, he died in Kirchstatten, Austria, where he is buried.

Louis MacNeice

Ulsterman Louis MacNeice (1907 to 1963) was at Marlborough before he went to Merton where he took a First in *Literae Humaniores* in 1930. MacNeice's contemporaries at Oxford included Spender, Auden and Day Lewis. This left-wing group called itself MacSpaunday from the first parts of each of its members' surnames.

He once climbed up on the college roof and dislodged a gargoyle which he then dropped through the ceiling of the Senior Common Room, startling the dons dozing away beneath him. Like generations of undergraduates before and after him, one of MacNeice's favourite haunts was the Perch by the river in the hamlet of Binsey. A description of his years at Merton is to be found in *Autumn Journal*

(1938), which criticises the limitations of a classical education.

After leaving Merton, MacNeice became a lecturer in Classics at Birmingham University and Bedford College, London, before going to the United States to lecture in English at Cornell University. On his return to Britain during World War II, he joined the BBC as a feature writer and producer.

The Bodleian Library owns a MacNeice archive, composed mainly of material from the period when he was writing for the BBC. The Library was able to save it from dispersal by purchasing it with financial assistance from a number of sources. The MacNeice archive joins those of several other writers with an Oxford connection, notably Joyce Cary, CS Lewis, Kenneth Grahame, JRR Tolkien, John Masefield and Edmund Crispin.

William Golding

Born in Cornwall, William Golding (1911 to 1993) was the son of a science master at Marlborough Grammar School where he went before coming up to Brasenose in 1930. He started his academic career by starting to read for a science degree, but changed course after two years and took a Second in English in 1934. As he had studied both physics and English literature at Marlborough, the change was not as drastic as it might sound. A diploma in Education which followed three years later enabled him to become a teacher.

Golding joined the Royal Navy in 1940 and saw active service during the Second World War. This period of his life affected his view of the world and gave him a cynical opinion of human nature. After the war, he worked from 1945 to 1962 as a teacher in Salisbury where he began to write. He published the books *Lord of the Flies* (1954), *The Inheritors* (1955), *Pincher Martin* (1956) and *Free Fall* (1959). *Lord of the Flies* was not, however, an immediate success and was rejected by

15 publishers. Golding is said to have written it after reading R M Ballantyne's schoolboy tale *The Coral Island*. From his own experience as a teacher, Golding did not believe that boys who had been shipwrecked would behave in such a gentlemanly way.

In 1983, he was awarded the Nobel Prize for Literature four months after he received an honorary D Litt from Oxford. Golding's portrait hangs in Brasenose College Hall.

Mollie Harris

The late Mollie Harris, who is perhaps better known outside Oxfordshire as Martha Woodford of *The Archers,* was brought up in Ducklington near Witney. Her first book, *A Kind of Magic* (1969), was an immediate best-seller, and other books on local customs and history written from Mollie's store of personal reminiscences followed. Later books were on Cotswold privies, local recipes and wine-making, including an Archers cookery book. Molly was a well-known character in and around Ducklington, Witney and Eynsham where she spent the later part of her life.

Barbara Pym

Barbara Mary Crampton Pym (1913 to 1980) was born in Shropshire at Oswestry, the daughter of a solicitor. She went to Huyton College in Liverpool and then on to St Hilda's where she gained a Second in English in 1934.

During the Second World War, she worked as a censor before joining the Women's Royal Naval Service. While working for the International African Institute from 1946 to 1974, she was assistant editor of the journal *Africa*.

Barbara Pym's *Some Tame Gazelle*, her first novel, appeared in 1950 and was followed by five more. She was discouraged from writing by the rejection of *An Unsuitable Attachment* in 1963 and *The Sweet Dove Died* six years later. She retired from the International African Institute in 1974 and, with her sister Hilary, came to live in Finstock, near Witney. In 1974, however, when a list was compiled by her fellow writers for the *Times Literary Supplement*, Pym was the only candidate to be nominated twice. Her *Quartet in Autumn* was a best seller and enabled her to publish more novels (both *Jane and Prudence* and *Crampton Hodnet* have Oxford connections), before she died of cancer in January 1980.

Miss Read

Miss Read is the pen name of Dora Jessie Saint who was born in 1913. Read was her mother's maiden name. She has written more than 40 novels many set in Thrush Green which is in reality Wood Green. This is the part of Witney which lies between the town centre and North Leigh. The area has some fine Cotswold stone houses and Holy Trinity church which was constructed in the 1840s to look after the spiritual needs of this expanding residential district. Previous to this, John Wesley preached a very successful open-air sermon on Wood Green.

The *Thrush Green* series is loosely based on 'Miss Read's' experiences as a village schoolteacher. The first of these novels, which was called simply *Thrush Green*, appeared in 1959, the last, *The Year at Thrush Green*, was published in 1995. The following year Dora Saint finished off her writing career with *A Peaceful Retirement*. She now lives across the county boundary at Shefford Woodlands in Berkshire.

Wood Green, Witney (Miss Read)

Dylan Thomas

Dylan Thomas (1914 to 1953) lodged for a time with his wife and family in a summerhouse in the grounds of Holywell Ford. They came for Christmas 1945 and stayed on to rent the summerhouse. While in Oxford, Thomas, who was by this time an alcoholic, became such a drain on his hostess, Margaret Taylor, wife of the historian AJP Taylor, that she found herself obliged to sell her Impressionist paintings in order to finance his addiction. His wife Caitlin said of her marriage 'I wouldn't have married him if he had not got the genius. He was too unattractive as a man.' While living at Holywell Ford, Thomas's favourite pub was the Port Mahon in St Clement's.

The Thomas family later moved to South Leigh, near Witney, where

Margaret Taylor bought the Manor House for them. The two years they spent there were not productive for the poet, as alcohol had taken over from his writing, he did not appreciate the help that he was given and his letters contain lists of complaints and disasters. Finally, the long suffering Mrs Taylor purchase the Boat House in Laugharne in Dylan Thomas's own South Wales where he spent the remainder of his days. He collapsed and died during a lecture tour of the USA.

Chapter Ten

Iris Murdoch ✍ John Bayley ✍ P D James ✍ Dick Francis

Edmund Crispin ✍ Philip Larkin ✍ Kingsley Amis

John Mortimer ✍ John Wain ✍ Nina Bawden

Elizabeth Jennings ✍ Colin Dexter ✍ David Cornwell

Lady Antonia Fraser ✍ Penelope Lively

Iris Murdoch

Iris Murdoch (1919 to 1999) went to Somerville where she got a First in *Literae Humaniores* in 1942. She was a Fellow of St Anne's from 1948 to 1963 and an honorary Doctorate of Literature followed in 1987. After that, she devoted her time entirely to writing, although from 1963 to 1967 she also lectured at the Royal College of Art. She wrote 26 novels in 40 years, the last, *Jackson's Dilemma*, when she had already got Alzheimer's. Because she was a perfectionist, Murdoch did not allow her editors to alter her text.

In 1956 she married John Bayley, six years her junior and himself an Oxford graduate, having got a First in English in 1950. He became Warton Professor of English and a Fellow of St Catherine's College from 1974 to 1992.

In John Bayley's biographical work, *Iris,* there are plenty of references to the city and it surroundings. The book starts with the Bayleys going out along the bypass and squeezing through a gap in the

St Antony's College (Iris Murdoch and John Bayley)

hedge, in order to go swimming in the river as they had done for almost 45 years.

When John Bayley first noticed Iris, he was gazing out of a window at St Antony's College where he then lived. Iris herself lived in a flat in Beaumont Street. She was 'bicycling slowly and rather laboriously past . . . '. He believes that he fell in love with her there and then. It was not, however, until they met at a social gathering at her own college, St Anne's, that he actually met her. Their first date was to a hop at St Antony's, preceded by dinner at the Regency Restaurant, which, says Bayley, 'advertised itself in the *Oxford Mail* as serving "probably the best food in Oxfordshire."' The experience was not a total success.

After Iris had decided that they should marry and had acquainted John with the fact, they were wed at the Registry Office which was at that time in St Giles'. Trips round the Oxfordshire countryside in search of somewhere to live followed, with possible houses being viewed in Bampton, Taynton and finally Steeple Aston where they moved into The Cedars.

The old house was cold, damp and somewhat primitive and the Bayleys' years of residence did nothing to improve its condition; by John's own admission they must have turned it into a sort of rural slum complete with resident rats. It did have the advantage of having a nature reserve for a garden and they enjoyed the wildlife around them, in particular the family of kingfishers which grew up there. After more than thirty years, the Cedars finally grew tired of them, confides Bayley, as if it could not wait for them to leave.

When they did, it was back to Oxford where John fell for a house in Summertown which he calls 54 Hartley Road, an address which does not exist. Despite Iris's obvious misgivings, the purchase went ahead but the expected Betjemanian joys of suburban living failed to materialise. As John Bayley puts it, 'the children round about screamed all day, and the neighbourhood burglars paid us routine visits at night.' After gritting their teeth for three years, the Bayleys moved to 30 Charlbury Road on the southern limits of North Oxford. According to John, they soon managed to redecorate this house with their own particular brand of neglect.

When her Altzheimer's had reached its final stage, Iris finally went into Vale House, a respite home, and died there several weeks later. By the time of her death, she had become, in her husband's words, like 'a very nice 3-year old.' The highly acclaimed film, *Iris*, starring Kate Winslet as the young writer, Dame Judi Dench as she was in her later years, and Jim Broadbent as John Bayley, was released in January 2002. In June that year, the Oxford Iris Murdoch Appeal was launched, it dual aims being to set up bursaries at St Anne's College for students who would not otherwise have been able to come to Oxford, and to endow a Professorship of Old Age Psychiatry.

P D James

P(hyllis) D(orothy) James (born 1920). The crime novelist was born in Oxford and left school at the age of 16. She had an assortment of jobs including assistant stage manager, nurse, mental health administrator and civil servant working in the criminal law department, most of which provided her with good experience for writing crime books. She wrote the first of these, *Cover Her Face*, published in 1962, while on the train to and from work.

Her most famous creation is Inspector Adam Dalgleish whose assistant is an Oxford graduate. Dalgleish's exploits have been turned into successful television programmes.

PD James was created a life peer (Baroness James of Holland Park), in 1991 and an honorary Fellow of St Hilda's in 1996. Her autobiography is entitled *A Time to be in Earnest*.

Dick Francis

Sir Richard Stanley Francis, better known as novelist and champion jockey Dick Francis, was born in 1920 in Tenby, South Wales, but went to school in Maidenhead, Berkshire. His name appears on the cover of many best-selling crime novels but his biography *Dick Francis a Racing Life* by Graham Lord relates how his wife, Mary, should receive at least half the credit as co-author. They were given a Dagger Award for *Whip Hand* in 1979 and Edgar Awards for *Forfeit* in 1970, *Whip Hand in* 1981 and *Come to Grief* in 1996.

In the early 1950s, the Francises bought fifty acres of land on the outskirts of Blewbury, a picturesque little village in the Vale of White Horse. Blewbury is surrounded by the Downs and in classic horse racing country. Penny Chase, as they called their new bungalow, took its name from the old adage, 'Take care of the pennies . . . '. Their home was very much in contrast with the mellow old buildings which formed much of the rest of Blewbury. Nevertheless they fell in love with it and spent 31 happy years there.

Mary and Dick Francis had a regular booking for Tuesday nights at the Oxford Playhouse. In 1960, their theatre-going provided an impetus for the first book, *Dead Cert*, when they made up their minds that they were able to write a novel which would be just as good as the play they had just seen.

Apart from the Playhouse, the citizens of Oxford were able to obtain glimpses of Dick Francis in the City Library, then in St Aldate's, and also at Kidlington airport where the couple kept two light aircraft which they leased out with a third, the Piper Cherokee Arrow, which Mary flew herself.

The Francises left Blewbury to live in America and then moved on to the Caribbean, where they intend to spend the rest of their lives on Grand Cayman, having even invested in two burial plots only a hundred yards or so from the sea.

Edmund Crispin

Edmund Crispin (1921 to 1978) is the pseudonym of Robert Bruce Montgomery. Born in Chesham Bois, Buckinghamshire, he went to St John's College where he took a Second in French and German in 1943. While he was still an undergraduate, his first novel, *The Case of the Gilded Fly*, was published by Gollancz. From 1943 to 1945, he taught at Shrewsbury School near to his college friend Philip Larkin.

Crispin's third book, *The Moving Toyshop* (1946), which is dedicated to Larkin, is considered one of the best of the early Oxford detective stories. The shop in the title commutes between the Iffley and the Banbury Roads.

Crispin provides a map which mixes genuine names (all the streets and Sheldonian, Trinity, St John's etc) with imaginary ones like the Mace and Sceptre and St Christopher's. The central character, Gervase Fen, was loosely based on Professor WE Moore, Professor of English Language and Literature. Fen is prone to using Latin quotations, such as *parturiunt montes nascetur ridiculus mus.*

Between 1944 and 1953, Crispin produced eight novels and established his reputation in the field of crime and mystery writing. In the mid-Forties, he also began a career as a professional musician under his own name, Bruce Montgomery. Already an accomplished pianist, organist and choirmaster, he composed songs, orchestral works and film scores, including several for the *Carry On* series. Music occupied much of his time, although he did produce a collection of short stories, entitled *Beware of the Train,* in 1953 and the final Gervase Fen story, *The Glimpses of the Moon,* in 1977. By this time, however, he had problems with alcohol and the associated lack of funds. Crispin died in September 1978.

St John's, Garden Front

Philip Larkin

Born in Coventry where his father was City treasurer, Philip Larkin (1922 to 1985) came up to St John's in 1940 and graduated three years later with a First in English. After an unsuccessful application to join the Civil Service, he became a librarian, firstly at the pubic library in Wellington, Shropshire. From there, he was able to keep in regular contact with his friend from St John's, the novelist Edmund Crispin (qv). During this period at Wellington, he was writing a novel as well as poetry. Posts in academic libraries at the Universities of Belfast and Leicester followed and from 1955 onwards Larkin was Librarian at the Brynmor Jones Library at the University of Hull.

Larkin edited *The Oxford Book of Twentieth-Century English Verse* (1973). In addition, he published two novels, *Jill* (1940), which is set in Oxford, and *A Girl in Winter* (1947); and two collections of critical pieces, *All What Jazz: A Record Diary, 1961–1968* (1970) and *Required Writing* (1983).

When he became deaf in the 1970s, Larkin stopped writing poetry and jazz criticism. Following the death of John Betjeman in 1984, he was offered the position of Poet Laureate, but turned it down. Larkin received an honorary D Litt from the University of Oxford in 1984, the year before his death.

Kingsley Amis

Kingsley Amis (1922 to 1995) was born in London, the only son of a business clerk. He was educated at the City of London School and came up to St John's in 1941 to read English. After service in the army with the Royal Corps of Signals, Amis completed his academic studies and worked as a lecturer in English at the University College of Swansea (1948–61) and in Cambridge (1961–63).

Amis made his debut as a novelist with *Lucky Jim* (1954), which was very successful. The comic main character also appeared in the novels *That Uncertain Feeling* (1956) and *I like it Here* (1958), a xenophobic novel set in Portugal. In the 1980s Amis wrote the Booker Prize winning novel *The Old Devils* (1986), which tells the story of a group of retired friends and their wives whose lives revolve around social drinking. *You can't do Both* (1994) was set between the wars, and told the story of Robin Davies, who progresses from south London suburbia, through Oxford, and on to a lectureship in a provincial university. Amis was knighted in 1990 – according to his son, Martin Amis, getting it partly for being 'audibly and visibly right-wing or conservative/monarchist.'

Amis died in 1995 at the age of 73 with more than 20 novels to his credit, plus dozens of volumes of poetry, stories, collections of essays, and criticism. Among the author's life-long friends was the poet Philip Larkin, whom Amis befriended because they were 'savagely uninterested in the same things.'

John Mortimer

John Mortimer (born 1923) came up to Brasenose from Harrow in 1940 when he was 17 and took a Third in Jurisprudence three years later. According to his own admission, his entrance 'examination' was farcical, consisting as it did of being handed a passage of Lucretius to translate at leisure. In this, Mortimer was helped by a friend and fellow applicant who appeared in the room carrying a Latin dictionary which he had just bought from Blackwell's. Between them, the two youngsters managed to write out a translation and set off to find the 'examiner' who was having lunch. Wordlessly, he took the translations and later they were both accepted. In fact, although they were both members of Brasenose, because that college was taken over by the War

Office they were sent off to Christ Church instead.

Strange as it may sound to the outsider, Oxford was Mortimer's first outing into the real world after what he calls the 'bizarre hothouse' of Harrow and it took him two years to come to terms with this. In wartime Oxford, the place to see and be seen in was still the George Restaurant, although during this period of austerity, under the Ministry of Food Regulations, the upper limit for the cost of a meal was five shillings and the steaks were made of whale meat.

Mortimer found the study of law, in theoretical terms, 'enormously dull' which may well account for the fact that, despite his obvious brainpower, he only managed a Third. He does point out that this was a war degree, obtained in the shortest time possible, a 'utility degree.'

A playwright, novelist and lawyer, Mortimer is best known today for the popular *Rumpole of the Bailey* television series starring Leo Mackern. Mortimer is himself a barrister, having been called to the bar in 1948 and becoming a QC in 1966. Knighted in 1998, Sir John Mortimer lives near Henley-on-Thames and is on the board of the Oxford Playhouse.

John Barrington Wain

John Barrington Wain (1925 to 1994) was born in Stoke-on-Trent where his father was a dentist. From Newcastle-under-Lyme Grammar School, he went up to St John's College where he took a First in English.

Between 1949 and 1955, he was a lecturer in English at the University of Reading after which he became a full-time freelance writer, an occupation he continued for the rest of his life. From 1973 to 1978, he was Professor of Poetry when he succeeded Roy Fuller.

The 1953 novel *Hurry on Down* (or *Born in captivity* as it was called in the United States) represents Wain's view of post-war Britain. It tells the story of Charles Lumley, an Oxford graduate who accepts menial employment in an attempt to 'find himself'. This caused Wain to be labelled, rather inaccurately, as an Angry Young Man along with Osborne, Braine and Sillitoe.

Wain won the Whitbread prize for 1982 with another novel, *Young shoulders*. In addition to fiction and poetry, he produced studies of other writers with a West Midlands background, notably Shakespeare, Johnson and Arnold Bennett, who, like Wain, came from Stoke.

Wain was associated with the Inklings as well as the post-war group of poets known as The Movement, which included DJ Enright, Thom Gunn and fellow Oxonians Kingsley Amis, Elizabeth Jennings and Philip Larkin. John Wain lived at Wolvercote and died there in May, 1974. The manuscripts of his work are in Edinburgh University Library.

Nina Bawden

Nina Bawden (born Nina Mabey in 1925) came to Oxford from Ilford County High School. She attended for interview at Somerville in her grammar school uniform and was understandably intimidated by what would now be called Sloane Rangers who were there for the same reason. The Principal, when Nina met her, was far less awe-inspiring, so that Nina found herself sufficiently relaxed to venture to criticise Wordsworth to Helen Darbishire, at that time the greatest expert on the poet. Nina was accepted by Somerville and subsequently changed faculties to read Modern Greats (Philosophy, Politics and Economics) instead of English. She remembers how one of her philosophy tutors, Dr MacKinnon of Keble, would sometimes roll on the floor and play with the coal in its scuttle, occasionally even chewing a lump while listening to her reading her essays out to him.

Nina's wartime Oxford included helping with the war effort by working as a waitress in the Red Cross Club in Beaumont Street and fire watching in museums and libraries.

There were no visits to the George. Instead, food was taken in college with occasional eating out at British Restaurants. In addition, there was the odd visit to the Taj Mahal in the Turl, Oxford's first (and for many years only) Indian restaurant, where a good lentil curry could be had for 9d.

Some of the highlights of Nina's years in Oxford were classic ones: falling in love with a male student at Carfax during the VE night celebrations; going to a dance at Queen's in a black taffeta dress; bathing naked in the river; skating on Port Meadow and going to the Classic cinema in Walton Street. And there was also something which few other people would be able to look back on, being invited out to tea by Richard Burton. At this time he was at Exeter College on a two-term short course and was appearing in Nevill Coghill's production of *Measure for Measure*. When they got there the teashop was closed, but they were served tea on a silver tray in the drawing room of the lady who lived next door.

Another celebrity-to-be, who was up at Oxford at the same time and also at Somerville, was Margaret Thatcher, fixed in the writer's memory as a plump, neat, solemn nineteen-year-old. Nina remembers criticising Thatcher's joining the Conservative Party and betraying her lower middle-class background. The future Prime Minister retorted that there was more chance of drawing attention to oneself among the Tories, as they were mainly 'a bit dull and stodgy' as Nina puts it.

Nina's last term was somewhat spoiled by the return of ex-servicemen from the War and these made the undergraduates feel like schoolchildren once more. Moreover, all their quiet familiar haunts were invaded by noisy strangers. On the other hand, this was compensated for by the influx of new and interesting people to the town. At this time too, Helen Darbishire retired and with her went an important part of Nina Bawden's Oxford. The writer herself left with a Second in PPE in 1946.

Elizabeth Jennings

The poet Elizabeth Jennings (born 1926), an adopted Oxonian, was born in Boston, Lincolnshire and started to write poetry when she was 13 years old. She went to Oxford High School and on to St Anne's College in 1944, where she took a 2nd in English in 1947. At this time, she came into contact with poets of The Movement. Some of her own early poems were published in *Oxford Poetry* in 1948; this was edited by Kingsley Amis and James Michie.

Elizabeth Jennings worked in Oxford City Library from 1950 to 1958 and as a reader for a publisher from 1958 to 1960.

Colin Dexter

Colin Dexter (born 1930) is a native of Stamford, in Lincolnshire. In 1950, he went up to Christ's College, Cambridge to read Classics after having completed his National Service with the Royal Corps of Signals. In 1954, he became an assistant classics master at Wyggeston School, Leicester. An appointment at Loughborough Grammar followed, before, in 1959, he took up the position of senior Classics master at Corby Grammar School in Northamptonshire. He spent 13 years teaching Latin and Greek before retiring from the profession because of increasing deafness. In 1966, his association with Oxford began when he accepted a position at the Oxford Local Examinations Board. Besides being the creator of 'Inspector Morse', Colin is a former British national crosswords champion and for many years set crosswords for *The Oxford Times.*

He created Inspector Morse while on a Welsh holiday with nothing better to do. There have been 13 Morse books, the first one appearing in 1975, and 33 programmes filmed for television, starring John Thaw in the title role with Kevin Whately as his sidekick, Sergeant Lewis.

Former City Library (Elizabeth Jennings)

Colin Dexter has himself appeared, à la Hitchcock, in 28 of these programmes.

It is not always easy for viewers to take in the fact that Inspector Morse is not a real person and the concept has been fostered by the media. The biographies of one hundred famous Oxonians, which *Newsquest Oxfordshire* produced for the Millennium, included an entry for Morse which ran:

Chief Insp Endeavour Morse 1930–1999
Policeman, opera lover, crossword addict, St John's College,
    Thames Valley Police, lived in North Oxford.

Morse, who came up to St John's to read Classics, was another of those Oxford men who failed to complete his course, having left after two years thanks to a disastrous love affair.

Morse, Twilight of the Gods (Colin Dexter)

Television programmes based upon Morse's personal escapades and professional exploits have brought Oxford and Oxfordshire to the attention of the world in a way nothing else had done for decades. During Morse's years with Thames Valley Police, the murder rate in Oxford rose so dramatically that it became the known as the homicide capital of Europe.

Colin's achievements as a writer have been recognised by several prestigious awards including the Crime Writers Association's Cartier Diamond Dagger in 1997, the greatest honour which can be bestowed on a crime writer. In addition, as *Newsquest's* 'Present Lives' points out, he has 'created an entire new tourist industry in Oxford'.

In an interview on October 2, 1999, he said 'I'm sad to see Morse go . . . but in the end it was the only way to end the era and I am quite content of the final result.' The final episode, *The Remorseful Day*, was the occasion for a farewell party in the prestigious Randolph Hotel which now has its own Morse Bar. Ironically, while fans were learning to come to terms with Morse's untimely demise, John Thaw died from cancer of the oesophagus in February 2002, aged only 60.

John le Carré

David Cornwell (born 1931), who is best known writing as John le Carré, was at Lincoln College where he got a First in German in 1956. After continuing his German studies at Berne University, he did his national service with the British Intelligence Corps in Austria. Cornwell resumed his education at Oxford in 1952 but was forced to leave the University and teach at Millford Junior School when his father went bankrupt in 1954.

A year later, he returned to Oxford and finally graduated in 1956 with a first-class degree. After an unhappy two-year stint teaching German at Eton, Cornwell tried a variety of jobs: in 1960, he joined the Foreign Office and, a year later, he was sent to Bonn as the second secretary to the British Embassy there. It was during this period that Cornwell published his first two novels, *Call for the Dead* (1961) *and A Murder of Quality* (1962), adopting the pseudonym John Le Carré because members of the Foreign Office did not publish under their own names.

Lady Antonia Fraser

Lady Antonia Fraser (now Lady Antonia Pinter) was born the Honorable Antonia Packenham in 1932 and brought up in North Oxford, where she went to the Dragon School. Both her parents have stood as Labour candidates for the City of Oxford.

In 1950, she went up to Lady Margaret Hall. Antonia is one of the

LMH Old Hall (Antonia Fraser)

few Members of the University whose memoirs dwell at any length on the process involved in actually sitting examinations at Oxford. For Antonia, this consists mainly of recollections of what she was wearing, in this case the compulsory uniform known as *sub fusc* which it is necessary to wear for exams and on certain other formal occasions, although these have become less frequent and in any case vary from college to college.

For girls *sub fusc* consists of black tights and shoes, black jacket and skirt or trousers and black tie, together with a white blouse. Antonia had her fantasies about this: 'Sheer black nylons with seams, a white transparent nylon blouse with billowing sleeves, a floppy black velvet artist's bow as tie?' She says that in her case this attempt at individuality didn't work, for the rules were strictly enforced. Nowadays, within the bounds of decency, they are interpreted fairly leniently.

Curiously, despite the fact that she claims to have been completely taken by surprise when the time for exams came upon her in the summer of 1953, Antonia does not mention the fact that she took a very creditable Second in Modern History.

Penelope Lively

Penelope Lively (born 1933) gained a Third in Modern History in 1954 from St Anne's College and later lived near Great Rollright. She won the Booker Prize in 1987 for *Moon Tiger* and was awarded an OBE two years later. Penelope Lively has written historical biographies as well as books for children.

Chapter Eleven

Alan Bennett ✍ *Jon Stallworthy* ✍ *Seamus Heaney*

Jeffrey Archer ✍ *Joanna Trollope* ✍ *Philip Pullman*

Humphrey Carpenter ✍ *Pam Ayres* ✍ *Ian McEwan*

Martin Amis ✍ *A N Wilson* ✍ *Margaret Frazer*

Alan Bennett

Dramatist and actor Alan Bennett (born 1934) came up to Exeter in 1954 from Leeds Modern School and took a First in Modern History in 1957. He held the position of temporary junior lecturer in history at Magdalen College from 1960 to 1962, during which period he began working on a D Phil on the royal retinue of Richard II. It was during his time at Oxford that he was able to develop his gift for both writing and performing sketches which poked fun at, among others, the Church, Royalty and the Establishment. In 1960, he joined forces with 3 other leading Oxbridge dramatic (and comic) talents, Dudley Moore from Magdalen and Peter Cook of Pembroke and Jonathan Miller of St John's College, both in Cambridge. The result was the groundbreaking *Beyond the Fringe* which had its debut at the Edinburgh Festival that year and was the vanguard of the satirical movement of the Sixties and Seventies.

Following the popularity of *Beyond the Fringe* and its trans-Atlantic success in 1962, Bennett decided against an academic life and launched himself into a career of writing revues and award winning plays for both stage and television.

More recent Bennett successes include his adaptation for television of *The Wind in the Willows* in 1991, for which he did the voice-over for Mole, and *The Madness of George III* which appeared the same year. Some scenes in the film version of *The Madness of King George* (which was made in 1995) were shot in Oxford.

Alan Bennett was made Honorary Fellow of Exeter in 1987 and a Doctorate of Literature from Leeds followed in 1990. Although he still lives in his native Yorkshire, he has by no means forgotten his old University despite the fact that he left Oxford in 1962. In 1993 he gave a performance of *Writing Home* in aid of the Bodleian Library's fund-raising campaign, and the Library was more than fortunate in securing his services for an evening in the Sheldonian Theatre as part of its quatercentenary celebrations in October 2002.

Jon Stallworthy

Jon Stallworthy (born 1935) went to the Dragon School in North Oxford and then on to Rugby and Magdalen where took a B Litt and won the Newdigate Prize for poetry in 1958, having been runner-up the previous year. He joined the Oxford University Press in 1959 and became Deputy Head of the Academic Division between 1975 and 1977. Various academic posts both at Oxford and elsewhere include a Visiting Fellowship at All Souls in 1971–2. One of Stallworthy's best-known works is the biography of Wilfred Owen which won the Duff Cooper Memorial Prize and the WH Smith Literary Award. In addition, he has edited the work of various other poets and been involved in the compilation of several anthologies of poems.

Jon Stallworthy is Professor of English Literature and Fellow of Wolfson College; he lives in the village of Old Marston on the outskirts of Oxford.

Seamus Heaney

Seamus Justin Heaney (born 1939) comes from County Derry. He went to Queen's College, Belfast and then became a lecturer in English.

The 'famous Seamus' as he is known in his native Ireland, has written verse about the political situation in his native country and reflections on Irish culture in general. Collections include *Death of a Naturalist* (1966), *Field Work* (1979), *and The Haw Lantern* (1987). *The Spirit Level* was chosen as the Whitbread Book of the Year in 1996, and *Opened Ground: Poems 1966–1996* appeared in 1998. His *Beowulf: A New Translation* (1999), a modern version of the Anglo-Saxon epic, also won the Whitbread Book of the Year award for which he beat his friend Ted Hughes. Seamus Heaney was Professor of Poetry at Oxford 1989–94 and was awarded the Nobel Prize for Literature in 1995. He is an honorary Fellow of Magdalen and St John's Colleges and received an honorary D Litt in 1997.

Jeffrey Archer

Jeffrey Archer (born 1940) is a native of Weston-super-Mare. A first-class runner, he took a Diploma from the Department of Education at Oxford where he trained to teach physical education and was attached to Brasenose College.

Archer became one of the country's youngest Members of Parliament (although not the very youngest as he has claimed) and established a high profile for himself. Then he was forced to resign his seat after some ill-advised investment moves. Unemployed and up to his ears in debt, he tried his hand at writing, his first efforts meeting with considerable success. The next book became a best seller in the United States and Archer was able to pay off his debts and negotiate some very lucrative book contracts.

This encouraged him to plan a return to politics and he positioned himself close to Margaret Thatcher, while the Conservative Party made the best of his celebrity status and used him as a crowd puller. These moves paid off and he rose to become Chairman of the Conservative Party. Scandal followed upon scandal and the rest is history, so that at the time of writing Lord Archer is serving a custodial sentence.

In 1990, his novel *Not a penny more, not a penny less,* which made him his second fortune, was filmed in Oxford. The book revolves around a scam in which a naive American business is given a bogus honorary degree from the University and the film included a mock-up of the Encaenia or honorary degree ceremony. The Chancellor was played by Sir John Geilgud and the film also starred Jenny Agutter, Ed Asner and Ed Begley junior.

Joanna Trollope

Joanna Trollope (born 1943), who also writes as Caroline Harvey, came up to St Hugh's College in 1962 where she got a Second in English in 1965. She sets her novel, *The Men and the Girls* (1992), in Oxford. One of the central characters, James Mallow, is driving along a dark and rainy Beaumont Street when he knocks off her bike a 'true Oxford spinster' complete with round spectacles, bag of books and a tin of cat food. By way of an apology, James takes the elderly lady, Beatrice Bachelor, to tea in the Randolph Hotel.

Beatrice lives not far away in Jericho's Cardigan Street, in the heart of *Jude the Obscure*'s Beersheba. James and his partner, Kate, live in the area too, but in the much more up-market Richmond Road.

Joss, Kate's daughter frequents the second hand clothes shops of Walton and Little Clarendon Streets, as well as patronising the local Pakistani corner shop where she buys her chewing gum.

Kate leaves James and moves out of Richmond Villa to live on Osney Island, not far from where Chaucer's Nicholas lodged in the Middle Ages. At first sight, she is entranced by Osney's cosmopolitan ambience as she strolls round South, East, West and Swan Streets. However, when she refuses to move in with the man who has supplanted James in her affections, he beats her up, and she goes to a women's hostel not far from St Margaret's church, only a short walk from Jericho. Eventually, the pull of Richmond Villa proves too strong to be ignored but. . .

In May 1993, Joanna Trollope delivered her first (and what she implied might be her last) sermon in Oriel College chapel; it was on the theme of self-fulfilment.

Philip Pullman

Philip Pullman (born 1946) is an East Anglian, born in Norwich. After travelling the world as part of a Royal Air Force family, he settled in North Wales where his English teacher influenced his schooldays.

In 1965, he went up to Exeter College where he read English and, after earning a living by an assortment of jobs, moved back to Oxford. He taught at several middle schools for 12 years and then went on to Westminster College where he became a part-time lecturer. His specialist subjects were the Victorian novel, folk stories and the study of the correlation between words and images. Eventually, he left teaching to become a full-time writer.

Pullman's first published novel was written for adults, although he had already done some children's writing in the course of his teaching career. *The Ruby in the Smoke,* Book 1 of the Sally Lockhart Trilogy, for example, is based on a play written for his young pupils.

The writer continues to live in Oxford where, like TE Lawrence, he writes in a specially adapted shed in his garden. This study houses a library, musical instruments and a man-sized rat which featured in the play *Sherlock Holmes and the Limehouse Horror.*

Pullman's main achievement to date is winning the prestigious 2001 Whitbread Book of the Year Prize, worth £30,000, for his novel *The Amber Spyglass* which forms the last part of the trilogy *His Dark Materials.* The first book, *The Golden Compass,* features a young orphan girl who is growing up in Oxford. In all, the trilogy took seven years of hard writing in the shed to complete.

It is most unusual for the winner of the children's book category to win the overall prize as Pullman did. In January 2000, JK Rowling won the category but was bested by Seamus Heaney. The film company, New Line, makers of *The Lord of the Rings,* has obtained the rights for *His Dark Materials.* The company plans to release the film of the first book within three years.

What Pullman likes best about living in Oxford is the ease of access to stimulating places like the Pitt Rivers Museum, with its anthropological collections, and the Bodleian Library, in which he feels it a privilege to work. Also high on the list of favourite places is Cutteslowe Park to the north of the city, which he finds ideal for relaxing and dog walking.

Humphrey Carpenter

Humphrey Carpenter (born 1946), the well-known radio presenter, lives in North Oxford and is the son of a former Bishop of Oxford. His writing ranges from the *Mr Majeika* series of books for children to children's drama, literary criticism and, above all, outstanding biographies of Auden, Tolkien, Britten and Archbishop Runcie.

Pam Ayres

Pam Ayres (born 1947) comes from Stanford-in-the-Vale, formerly in Berkshire. When she left school Pam went into the Civil Service and then joined the Women's Royal Air Force where she was able to develop her talent for acting and singing. It was at this period that the idea of becoming a professional entertainer was conceived.

On her return to Oxfordshire, she took a job working as a secretary at Smith's Electrical Company in Witney. As soon as she could, Pam started to further her career in the world of entertainment by performing at the folk club at Ducklington, near Witney. In 1974, she progressed to reading one of her poems on BBC Radio Oxford, an opportunity which led to further broadcasts.

Pam made several unsuccessful attempts at getting her poems published commercially and finally decided to publish them herself. The title of this groundbreaking volume was *The Entire Collection (Eight) of Masterpieces by Pam Ayres, Famous Poet and Washer of Jam jars,* and it sold well in West Oxfordshire.

The following year, after much encouragement, she made her name on the television talent show *Opportunity Knocks,* again reciting poems which she had written herself. Typical Ayres titles are *I wish I'd looked after my Teeth; Like You Would* and *The Embarrassing Experience with the Parrot.*

She has had her own television series, *The World of Pam Ayres,* and has published several volumes of poetry, many of the poems having been recorded on cassettes and discs for which she has received silver, gold and platinum discs. One of the many highlights of her career was the Silver Jubilee Royal Variety Performance at the London Palladium, as well as a series of concert tours of Australia, the Middle East, Hong Kong, Canada and New Zealand.

Further volumes of poetry were published in the conventional way, as well as many children's books, one of which has been translated into Japanese.

Ian McEwan

Ian McEwan (born 1948) was Cameron Mackintosh Professor of Theatre based at St Catherine's College. He won the Booker Prize for his novel *Enduring Love,* the start of which describes a ballooning accident in the Chilterns.

Martin Amis

Martin Amis (born 1949) is another native Oxonian, his father, Kingsley Amis being a doctoral student at the University at the time of Martin's birth. He spent his boyhood wherever his father was teaching, first in Swansea and later at Princeton, before coming back to England to live in Cambridge. When Martin was twelve his parents divorced and he went off for a year to live in Majorca with his mother, sister and brother. On his return to England, he made a film called *A High Wind in Jamaica,* and finished his schooling at 'crammers' where he never managed to do well academically. One headmaster even stated that Amis was 'unusually unpromising.'

When Martin was introduced to the works of Jane Austen, however, all this changed and he was motivated to study for Oxford entrance. In 1968 he came up to Exeter College, where, by his own admission, he spent the next three years trying to convince himself that he really was an Oxford student. In *The Rachel Papers,* he writes of Oxford, 'never knew a place so full of itself.' Nevertheless, he graduated with a First in English Language and Literature.

After he left Oxford, Martin Amis worked as book reviewer for the *Observer* and subsequently held a series of editorial positions in the course of the next eight years, notably for the *Times Literary Supplement, the New Statesman,* and *the Observer,* where he has been special writer since 1980.

A N Wilson

Andrew (AN) Wilson (born 1950) has been Literary Editor of the *Evening Standard* since 1990. While at New College, he won the Chancellor's Essay Prize in 1971 and the Ellerton Theological Prize. For a short while in the early Seventies he worked in the Periodicals department of J Thornton and Son's bookshop in Broad Street, then went on to be a lecturer at St Hugh's and New Colleges.

In *The Healing Art,* he describes the 'damp English scene' in Jericho with St Barnabas's 'Venetian water-tower,' the city's scruffy Edwardian shops and the 'cube of black glass' which forms part of BH Blackwell's offices in Hythe Bridge Street, as well as the traditional pinnacles and spires, domes and buttresses and the hidden quads and secret places of the colleges.

Margaret Frazer

Margaret Frazer is the pen name of the partnership of Gail Frazer and Mary Monica Pulver Kuhfeld, which has produced several prize-winning books set in medieval Oxfordshire. Although the latter writer has opted out of the venture, Mrs Frazer continues. The duo produced six books, including *The Servant's Tale* and *The Bishop's Tale,* as well as two award nominations before they went their separate ways.

The Novice's Tale, 'the first in a history mystery series' as Frazer calls it, is set in the small mid-15th century Benedictine community of St Frideswide's, somewhere in the Oxfordshire countryside. The heroine is called Frevisse, a well-researched choice of name as it is the French equivalent of Frideswide. This religious foundation would not appear to be the real St Frideswide's Priory (the forerunner of Christ Church Cathedral), an Augustinian house which was situated near the heart of the medieval town.

'Margaret Frazer's' books have not been published in England and do not appear in the OLIS catalogue of the Bodleian Library.

✍   ✍   ✍   ✍   ✍

As has been noted, Oxfordshire authors fall into several categories. The most obvious are those members of the University who have a degree in English Language and Literature and who have been trained to study other writers and to organise their own thoughts and output. Because of the late introduction of English Language and Literature into the Oxford syllabus these authors date only from the last century and became more numerous as the 20th century progressed.

Other graduates have degrees in modern or classical languages and literatures and will have undergone tuition similar to those of the English specialists. A third category includes those who have studied an entirely different discipline such as mathematics or medicine.

Some Oxford graduates stayed for the rest of their lives, others left it but continued to keep in touch, while the rest came back seldom or not at all. More common than might be expected are those who started off their academic careers at Oxford but for a variety of reasons either did not receive a degree or failed to take one at all. Some of those who left the University did so of their own free will, while others had no choice. It must be borne in mind that, until well into the 19th century with the arrival of a substantial number of middle class students, academic study and passing examinations played little part in Oxford life. To the upper classes and the nobility, a university was an important place in which to meet and mix with members of one's own class and background, and to make contacts which would last a lifetime. This attitude lasted into the 20th century. Not counting those who were sent down, writers who left Oxford without a degree include the metaphysical poet Henry Vaughan, Samuel Johnson, Robert Southey and Max Beerbohm.

Then there are those with no existing Oxfordshire connections who either came to visit, work or to make the city their home and decided to stay on. A leading example is Colin Dexter who is said be the best thing that has happened to the Oxford tourist industry for decades.

Last, but certainly not least, there are the true natives of Oxfordshire who have managed to inject into their writing a real flavour of the County.

Index of Writers

Index of County Place Names
(excluding central Oxford)

Books published by
THE BOOK CASTLE

EXPLORING HISTORY ALL AROUND *Vivienne Evans* Planned as seven circular car tours, plus background to places of interest en-route in Bedfordshire and parts of Bucks and Herts.

COUNTRYSIDE CYCLING IN BEDFORDSHIRE, BUCKINGHAMSHIRE AND HERTFORDSHIRE *Mick Payne* Twenty rides on and off-road for all the family.

PUB WALKS FROM COUNTRY STATIONS: Bedfordshire and Hertfordshire
Clive Higgs Fourteen circular country rambles, each starting and finishing at a railway station and incorporating a pub stop at a mid way point.

PUB WALKS FROM COUNTRY STATIONS: Buckinghamshire and Oxfordshire
Clive Higgs Circular rambles incorporating pub-stops.

LOCAL WALKS: South Bedfordshire and North Chilterns *Vaughan Basham* Twenty-seven thematic circular walks.

LOCAL WALKS: North and Mid Bedfordshire *Vaughan Basham* Twenty-five thematic circular walks.

FAMILY WALKS: Chilterns South *Nick Moon*
FAMILY WALKS: Chilterns North *Nick Moon*
Two books each containing thirty shorter circular walks.

CHILTERN WALKS: Hertfordshire, Bedfordshire and North Bucks *Nick Moon*
CHILTERN WALKS: Buckinghamshire *Nick Moon*
CHILTERN WALKS: Oxfordshire and West Buckinghamshire *Nick Moon*
A trilogy of collections of circular walks, in association with the Chiltern Society. Each volume contains 30 circular walks.

OXFORDSHIRE WALKS Oxford, the Cotswolds and the Cherwell Valley *Nick Moon*
OXFORDSHIRE WALKS Oxford, the Downs and the Thames Valley *Nick Moon*
Two volumes that complement Chiltern Walks: Oxfordshire, and complete coverage of the county, in association with the Oxford Fieldpaths Society. Thirty circular walks in each.

THE D'ARCY DALTON WAY *Nick Moon* Long-distance footpath across the Oxfordshire Cotswolds and Thames Valley, with various circular walk suggestions.

THE CHILTERN WAY *Nick Moon* The authorised guide to the new 133 mile circular Long-Distance-Path through Bedfordshire, Buckinghamshire, Hertfordshire and Oxfordshire, as planned by the Chiltern Society.

JOURNEYS INTO BUCKINGHAMSHIRE *Anthony Mackay* Superb line drawings plus background text: large format landscape gift book.

COCKNEY KID AND COUNTRYMEN *Ted Enever* The Second World War remembered by the children of Woburn Sands and Aspley Guise.

CHANGING FACES, CHANGING PLACES: Post war Bletchley and Woburn Sands 1945–1970 *Ted Enever* Evocative memoirs of post-war life on the Beds/Bucks borders, up to the coming of Milton Keynes new town.

BUCKINGHAM AT WAR *Pip Brimson* Stories of courage, humour and pathos as Buckingham people adapt to war.

WINGS OVER WING: The Story of a World War 11 Bomber Training Unit
Mike Warth The activities of RAF Wing in Buckinghamshire.

HISTORIC FIGURES IN THE BUCKINGHAMSHIRE LANDSCAPE *John Houghton* Major personalities and events that have shaped the county's past, including a special section on Bletchley Park.

TWICE UPON A TIME *John Houghton* N. Bucks short stories loosely based on fact.

SANCTITY AND SCANDAL IN BEDS AND BUCKS *John Houghton* A miscellany of unholy people and events.

MANORS and MAYHEM, PAUPERS and PARSONS: Tales from Four Shires: Beds., Bucks., Herts. and Northants *John Houghton* Little known historical snippets and stories.

BUCKINGHAMSHIRE MURDERS *Len Woodley* Nearly two centuries of nasty crimes.

THE LAST PATROL: Policemen killed on duty while serving the Thames Valley *Len Woodley*

UNEXPLAINED OXFORD AND OXFORDSHIRE *Marilyn Yurdan* The unexplained in all its guises in one of the country's most historic towns and the villages of the rest of the county.

CHANGES IN OUR LANDSCAPE: Aspects of Bedfordshire, Buckinghamshire and the Chilterns 1947–1992 *Eric Meadows* Over 350 photographs from the author's collection spanning nearly 50 years.

JOURNEYS INTO BEDFORDSHIRE *Anthony Mackay* Foreword by The Marquess of Tavistock, Woburn Abbey. A lavish book of over 150 evocative ink drawings.

FOLK: Characters and Events in the History of Bedfordshire and Northamptonshire *Vivienne Evans* Anthology of people of yesteryear – arranged alphabetically by village or town.

JOHN BUNYAN: His Life and Times *Vivienne Evans* Highly praised and readable account.

A LASTING IMPRESSION *Michael Dundrow* A boyhood evacuee recalls his years in the Chiltern village of Totternhoe near Dunstable.

AGAINST THE ODDS: A passion for the country *Michael Dundrow* An intriguing imaginative sequel to his previous book.

ELEPHANTS I'LL NEVER FORGET: A Keeper's Life at Whipsnade and London Zoo *John Weatherhead* Experiences, dramatic and sad, from a lifetime with these well-loved giants.

WHIPSNADE MY AFRICA *Lucy Pendar* The inside story of sixty years of this world-renowned institution. Full of history, anecdotes, and animal stories.

GLEANINGS REVISITED: Nostalgic Thoughts of a Bedfordshire Farmer's Boy *E. W. O'Dell* A lively account of rural Bedfordshire in days gone by.

THREADS OF TIME *Shela Porter* The life of a remarkable mother and businesswoman, spanning the entire century and based in Hitchin and (mainly) Bedford.

HARLINGTON HEYDAYS AND HIGHLIGHTS *Edna L. Wilsher* One of Bedfordshire's most historic villages, Harlington's yesteryears are seen through the eyes of one of its most empathetic residents.

FLITWICK: A DAILY TONIC *Keith Virgin* Written as a "Book of Days" containing extracts from the Flitwick Parish Magazine and local newspapers of around 100 years ago.

FARM OF MY CHILDHOOD, 1925–1947 *Mary Roberts* An almost vanished lifestyle on a remote farm near Flitwick.

BEDFORDSHIRE'S YESTERYEARS: The Rural Scene *Brenda Fraser-Newstead* Vivid first-hand accounts of country life two or three generations ago.

BEDFORDSHIRE'S YESTERYEARS: Craftsmen and Tradespeople
Brenda Fraser-Newstead Fascinating recollections over several generations practising many vanishing crafts and trades

BEDFORDSHIRE'S YESTERYEARS: War Times and Civil Matters
Brenda Fraser-Newstead Two World Wars, plus transport, law and order, etc.

DUNSTAPLELOGIA *Charles Lamborn* Facsimile of a well-respected mid-Victorian town history, with a number of engravings of local buildings.

DUNNO'S ORIGINALS A facsimile of the rare pre-Victorian history of Dunstable and surrounding villages. New preface and glossary by John Buckledee, Editor of The Dunstable Gazette.

DUNSTABLE DOWN THE AGES *Joan Schneider and Vivienne Evans* Succinct overview of the town's prehistory and history – suitable for all ages.

HISTORIC INNS OF DUNSTABLE *Vivienne Evans* Illustrated booklet, especially featuring ten pubs in the town centre.

PROUD HERITAGE: A Brief History of Dunstable, 1000–2000AD *Vivienne Evans* Century by century account of the town's rich tradition and key events, many of national significance.

DUNSTABLE WITH THE PRIORY: 1100–1550 *Vivienne Evans*
Dramatic growth of Henry 1's important new town around a major crossroads.

DUNSTABLE IN TRANSITION: 1550–1700 *Vivienne Evans* Wealth of original material as the town evolves without the Priory.

HENRY VIII's DUNSTABLE *Vivienne Evans* Booklet telling of the king's association with the town.

DUNSTABLE DECADE: THE EIGHTIES: A Collection of Photographs *Pat Lovering*
A souvenir book of nearly 300 pictures of events in the 1980s.

STREETS AHEAD: An Illustrated Guide to the Origins of Dunstable's Street Names
Richard Walden Fascinating text and captions to hundreds of photographs, past and present, throughout the town.

DUNSTABLE IN DETAIL *Nigel Benson* A hundred of the town's buildings and features, plus town trail map.

DUNSTAPLE: A Tale of The Watling Highway *A. W.Mooring* Dramatic novelisation of Dunstable's legend of Dunne the Robber – reprinted after a century out of print.

25 YEARS OF DUNSTABLE:. A photographic treasure-trove of the town up to the Queen's Silver Jubilee, 1952–1977 *Bruce Turvey*

DUNSTABLE SCHOOL: 1888–1971 *F.M.Bancroft* Short history of one of the town's most influential institutions.

STRIKE UP THE BAND: Two centuries of music in Dunstable & District *Tony Ward*
Visual presentation of the stories behind the many local bands.

BOURNE and BRED: A Dunstable Boyhood Between the Wars *Colin Bourne*
Elegantly written, well illustrated book capturing the spirit of the town over fifty years ago.

OLD HOUGHTON *Pat Lovering* Pictorial record capturing the changing appearances of Houghton Regis over the past 100 years.

ROYAL HOUGHTON *Pat Lovering* Illustrated history of Houghton Regis from the earliest of times to the present.

WERE YOU BEING SERVED?: Remembering 50 Luton Shops of Yesteryear
Bob Norman Well-illustrated review of the much loved, specialist outlets of a generation or two ago.

THE STOPSLEY BOOK *James Dyer* Definitive, detailed account of this historic area of Luton. Includes 150 rare photographs.

THE STOPSLEY PICTURE BOOK *James Dyer* A wealth of new material and photographs make an ideal companion to The Stopsley Book.

PUBS and PINTS: The Story of Luton's Public Houses and Breweries *Stuart Smith* The background to beer in the town, plus hundreds of photographs, old and new.

LUTON AT WAR – VOLUME ONE As compiled by the Luton News in 1947, a well illustrated thematic account.

LUTON AT WAR – VOLUME TWO Second part of the book compiled by The Luton News. New index by James Dyer to both volumes.

THE CHANGING FACE OF LUTON: An Illustrated History *Stephen Bunker, Robin Holgate and Marian Nichols* Luton's development from earliest times to the present busy, industrial town.

WHERE THEY BURNT THE TOWN HALL DOWN: Luton, The First World War and the Peace Day Riots, July 1919 *Dave Craddock* Detailed analysis of a notorious incident.

THE MEN WHO WORE STRAW HELMETS: Policing Luton, 1840–1974
Tom Madigan Fine chronicled history, many rare photographs; author served in Luton Police for fifty years.

BARKING MAD: Cautionary Tails! *Danae Johnston* The humorous exploits of two delinquent poodles. A must for dog lovers.

A BRAND NEW BRIGHT TOMORROW . . . A Hatters Promotional Diary
Caroline Dunn A fans account of Luton Town Football Club during the successful 2001–2002 season.

COMPLETELY TOP HATTERS: Luton Town F.C. – An A–Z of major players, matches and records *Dean Hayes* Stars and incidents throughout the good days and not so good in the club's history.

KENILWORTH SUNSET: A Luton Town Supporter's Journal *Tim Kingston* Frank and funny account of the club's ups and downs.

A HATTER GOES MAD! *Kristina Howells* Luton Town footballers, officials and supporters talk to a female fan.

LEGACIES: Tales and Legends of Luton and the North Chilterns *Vic Lea* Mysteries and stories based on fact, including Luton Town Football Club. Many photographs.

JOURNEYS INTO HERTFORDSHIRE *Anthony Mackay* A foreword by The Marquis of Salisbury, Hatfield House. Introducing nearly 200 superbly detailed line drawings.

STICKS AND STONES: The Life and Times of a Journeyman Printer in Hertford, Dunstable, Cheltenham and Wolverton *Harry Edwards*

SUGAR MICE AND STICKLEBACKS: Childhood Memories of a Hertfordshire Lad
Harry Edwards Vivid evocation of gentle pre-war in an archetypal village, Hertingfordbury.

CRIME IN HERTFORDSHIRE Volume 1 Law and Disorder *Simon Walker* Authoritative survey of the changing legal process over many centuries.

CRIME IN HERTFORDSHIRE Volume 2 Murder and Misdemeanours *Simon Walker* Well researched, detailed murder cases.

BETWEEN THE HILLS: The Story of Lilley, a Chiltern Village *Roy Pinnock* A priceless piece of our heritage – the rural beauty remains but the customs and way of life described here have largely disappeared.

THE LILLEY PICTURE BOOK *Betty Shaw* A picture book depicting village activities during the late nineteenth century and mainly the twentieth century.

HARE AND HOUNDS: The Aldenham Harriers *Eric Edwards* Detailed highly illustrated history of a countryside institution based in Bedfordshire, Buckinghamshire and Hertfordshire.

THE HILL OF THE MARTYR: An Architectural History of St.Albans Abbey *Eileen Roberts* Scholarly and readable chronological narrative history of Hertfordshire and Bedfordshire's famous cathedral. Fully illustrated with photographs and plans.

MYSTERIOUS RUINS: The Story of Sopwell, St.Albans *Donald Pelletier* Still one of the town's most atmospheric sites. Sopwell's history is full of fluctuations and interest, mainly as a nunnery associated with St.Albans Abbey.

HAUNTED HERTFORDSHIRE *Nicholas Connell and Ruth Stratton* Ghosts and other mysterious occurrences throughout the county's market towns and countryside.

LEAFING THROUGH LITERATURE: Writers' Lives in Herts and Beds *David Carroll* Illustrated short biographies of many famous authors and their connections with these counties.

A PILGRIMAGE IN HERTFORDSHIRE *H.M.Alderman* Classic, between-the-wars tour round the county, embellished with line drawings.

THE VALE OF THE NIGHTINGALE *Molly Andrews* Several generations of a family, lived against a Harpenden backdrop.

SWANS IN MY KITCHEN *Lis Dorer* Story of a Swan Sanctuary at Hemel Hempstead.

THE TALL HITCHIN INSPECTOR'S CASEBOOK: A Victorian Crime Novel Based on Fact *Edgar Newman* Worthies of the time encounter more archetypal villains.

Specially for Children

VILLA BELOW THE KNOLLS: A Story of Roman Britain *Michael Dundrow* An exciting adventure for young John in Totternhoe & Dunstable two thousand years ago.

THE RAVENS: One Boy Against the Might of Rome *James Dyer* On the Barton Hills and in the south-east of England as the men of the great fort of Ravensburgh (near Hexton) confront the invaders.

Titles acquired by THE BOOK CASTLE

A BEDFORDSHIRE QUIZ BOOK *Eric Meadows* Wide ranging quizzes and picture puzzles on the history, people, places and bygones of the county.

CURIOSITIES OF BEDFORDSHIRE: A County Guide to the Unusual *Pieter and Rita Boogaart* Quirky well-illustrated survey of little-known features in the county.

BEDFORDSHIRE WILDLIFE *B.S.Nau, C.R.Boon, J.P.Knowles for the Bedfordshire Natural History Society* Over 200 illustrations, maps, photographs and tables survey the plants and animals of this varied habitat.

THE BIRDS OF BEDFORDSHIRE *Paul Trodd and David Kramer* Environments, breeding maps and details of 267 species, with dozens of photographs, illustrations and diagrams.

THE BIRDS OF HERTFORDSHIRE *Tom Gladwin and Bryan Sage* Essays, maps and records for all 297 species, plus illustrations, photographs and other plates.

THE BUTTERFLIES OF HERTFORDSHIRE *Brian Sawford* History and ecological guide, with colour photographs and maps for nearly 50 species.

WELWYN RAILWAYS *Tom Gladwin, Peter Neville, Douglas White* A history of the Great Northern line from 1850 to 1986, as epitomised by the five-mile stretch between Welwyn Garden City and Woolmer Green. Profusely illustrated in colour and black and white – landscape format.

THE LIFE AND TIMES OF THE GREAT EASTERN RAILWAY (1839–1922) *Harry Paar and Adrian Gray* Personalities, accidents, traffic and tales, plus contemporary photographs and old o.s.maps of this charming railway that transformed East Anglia and Hertfordshire between 1839 and 1922.

THE QUACK *Edgar Newman* Imaginative faction featuring characters in a nineteenth-century painting of a Hitchin market scene – especially quack doctor William Mansell.

D-DAY TO ARNHEIM – with Hertfordshire's Gunners *Major Robert Kiln* Vivid, personal accounts of the D-Day preparations and drama, and the subsequent Normandy battles, plus photographs and detailed campaign maps.

Chiltern Footpath Maps

No.1 High Wycombe and Marlow
No.2 Henley and Nettlebed
No.3 Wendover and Princes Risborough
No.4 Henlet and Caversham
No.5 Sarratt and Chipperfield
No.6 Amersham and Penn Country
No.7 West Wycombe and P.Risborough
No.8 Chartridge and Cholesbury
No.9 The Oxfordshire Escarpment
No.10 Wallingford and Watlington
No.11 The Hambledon Valley
No.12 Hughenden Valley and Great Missenden

No.13 Beaconsfield and District
No.14 Stokenchurch and Chinnor
No.15 Crowmarsh and Nuffield
No.16 Goring and Mapledurham
No.17 Chesham and Berkhamsted
No.18 Tring and Wendover
No.19 Ivinghoe and Ashridge
No.20 Hemel Hempstead and the Gade Valley
No.21 Dunstable Downs and Caddington
No.22 Gerrards Cross and Chalfont St.Peter
No.23 Toddington and Houghton Regis

All the above are available via any bookshop, or from the publisher and bookseller
THE BOOK CASTLE , 12 Church Street, Dunstable, Bedfordshire, LU5 4RU
Tel (01582) 605670   Fax (01582) 662431
Email bc@book-castle.co.uk   Website www.book-castle.co.uk

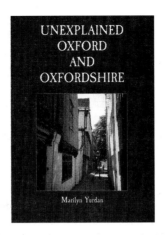

UNEXPLAINED OXFORD AND OXFORDSHIRE
Marilyn Yurdan

Unexplained Oxford and Oxfordshire is the result of several years of collecting strange stories and folk tales from all over the county, including the vale of White Horse which was transferred from Berkshire in 1974. As befits a part of the country which has been at the cross roads of human activity from prehistoric times onwards, there has been no shortage of material, and haunted sites in Oxfordshire range from the conventionally creepy to the modern council house, and sightings vary from vague, unidentified shapes to recognisable local characters.

The majority of the accounts covered by the book have been taken from the extensive "Ghost File" of Oxford and County Newspapers, others have been told directly to the author and the rest are part of the rich and ancient folklore of Oxfordshire. Three of the extraordinary happenings recorded in the book took place when Marilyn was present, and she is always interested in hearing from other people about similar experiences.

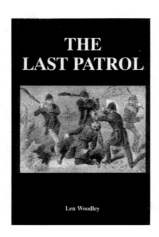

THE LAST PATROL
Policemen Killed on Duty while Serving in the Thames Valley

Len Woodley

This book details those Policemen who have been killed on duty by a criminal act within the area now covered by the Thames valley Police – namely the counties of Berkshire, Buckinghamshire and Oxfordshire. It ranges from a Constable who, in the 1860s, died in Oxford just days after the formation of one of the constituent forces that made up the present-day Thames Valley Police and must surly be one of the shortest serving Policemen in this country, to the truly terrible day at Hungerford in the late 1980s, when so many people, including a traffic Constable, were murdered and others wounded in that picturesque Berkshire town. It encompasses Police officers encountering poachers, ejecting some drunken men from a public house, checking details of members of the visiting forces involved in a fracas in wartime England, attempting the apprehension of burglars and questioning some vicious, "stop at nothing" criminals over their behaviour in a motor car.

These police officers all started their day as normal, not one gave a thought to the possibility that he might be sent to a life-threatening job.

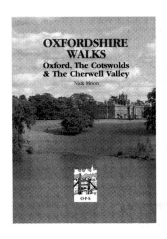
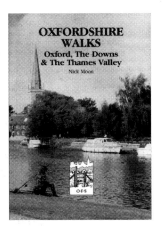

OXFORDSHIRE WALKS VOLUME 1
Oxford , The Cotswolds & The Cherwell Valley
&
OXFORDSHIRE WALKS VOLUME 2
Oxford,The Downs & The Thames Valley

Nick Moon

Two titles each containing thirty circular walks. The two titles together provide a comprehensive coverage of walks throughout the whole of Oxfordshire (except the Chiltern part already covered in "Chiltern Walks: Oxfordshire and West Buckinghamshire" by the same author). The walks vary in length from 3.3 to 12.0 miles, but the majority are in, or have options in, the 5 to 7 miles range, popular for half-day walks, although suggestions of possible combinations of walks are given for those preferring a full day's walk.

Each walk gives details of nearby places of interest and is accompanied by a specially drawn map of the route, which also indicates local pubs and a skeleton road network.

CHILTERN WALKS
Oxfordshire and West Buckinghamshire

Nick Moon

This book is one of a series of three to provide a comprehensive coverage of walks throughout the whole of the Chiltern area (as defined by the Chiltern Society). The walks included vary in length from 3.0 to 10.9 miles, but are mainly in the 5–7 mile range popular for half-day walks, although suggestions of possible combinations of walks are given for those preferring a full day's walk.

Each walk gives details of nearby places of interest and is accompanied by a specially drawn map of the route which also indicates local pubs and a skeleton road network.